HIDDEN
HISTORY
of
BOONE COUNTY,
INDIANA

HIDDEN
HISTORY
of
BOONE COUNTY,
INDIANA

Heather Phillips Lusk

THE
History
PRESS

Published by The History Press
Charleston, SC
www.historypress.com

Copyright © 2022 by Heather Phillips Lusk
All rights reserved

First published 2022

Manufactured in the United States

ISBN 9781467150224

Library of Congress Control Number: 2021952414

*To all those whose small contributions
make a large impact on the world.*

CONTENTS

CONTENTS

ACKNOWLEDGEMENTS

I can't fathom how a book like this could properly come into being without the assistance of so many people. First and foremost, thank you to those who came before and their attempts to capture and preserve history. Newspaper editors like Calton Gault and Strange Cragun reported local events and filled gaps when they were able. Their interviews with some of the first Boone County settlers provided incredible information. Writers for the *Boone County Magazine* nearly fifty years ago did much of the legwork, putting some of these stories together while their subjects were still alive. None of this would have been possible without the work of Ralph Stark, who compiled a massive amount of research.

Those who are currently ensuring county history is maintained are equally appreciated. Eric Spall, Boone County historian, set me on the right path with my endeavors to learn about county history and guided me to find the accurate answers in this book. Jane Hammock, Cynthia Young, Sandy Naekel, Rick Mitchell, Tom Wethington, Bill Leeke and Kristina Huff shared so much helpful information and provided access to resources. These people keep history alive, and organizations like SullivanMunce Cultural Center, Thorntown Heritage Museum, Jackson Township Historical Society and Boone County Historical Society keep it safe.

I sincerely appreciate Missy Krulik, the Howden family, the Spees family, Cindy Lamberjack, Sally Tanselle, Ralph Stacy, Nicole Kobrowski and Gary Essary, who led me to some amazing stories and helped to fill in the blanks. Thank you also to Harley Sheets, to David Brown and to Debbie and Greg

ACKNOWLEDGEMENTS

McGrath, who gave me access to their private collections. *Neewe* to George Ironstack, who provided wisdom and education to help me tell the history of the Eel River band that needed to be told.

The work couldn't have been accomplished without the support of friends like Megan Moosbrugger, Alysia Diffendal and Donna Phillips, who helped proofread chapters and ensure I was clearly recounting these stories. Above all else, thank you to my mother, and my husband and our daughters.

Were it not for my mother's love and appreciation of Native American history and culture, the Eel River band's story might not exist in these pages. Many years ago, I tried to find information about the first people who lived in Boone County. There was little that had been written, surprising considering a reservation filled one quarter of Boone County for more than a decade. Learning more about them was in the back of my mind as I became involved in local history and the SullivanMunce Cultural Center. That's where I discovered tales of other individuals whose lives left a mark on the county. As a journalist, I'm confident that every person has a story to tell; the challenge is finding that story when the subject is no longer among us to tell it themselves.

There are many, many more stories than those that lie within these pages. This is simply a drop in the bucket to share some of Boone County's hidden history.

PART I.

THE SHAPING OF BOONE COUNTY

CHAPTER 1

THE NATIVE AMERICAN INFLUENCE

Several hundred years ago, central Indiana was mostly swampland, thickly covered with trees and brush. Boone County, located at the geographic center of the state, was no different. The county seat of Lebanon was only selected because of its central location and not at all because of the ease of developing it.

The county's name is credited by the Indiana General Assembly "in honor of Colonel Daniel Boone, the pioneer of the west." Only a true pioneer would brave such unpleasant territory. Mosquitos, frogs, deer, bears and other wildlife dominated the area, and much of the land was deemed uninhabitable.

It's an image that is challenging to conjure today. Boone County in 2021 is 85 percent farmland, with 94 percent of the farms being family-owned. Early settlers made use of channels and ditches, and over time the county incorporated more than one thousand miles of drainage tiles to divert water in order to create livable land. Today the evidence of these efforts is subtle, but the result is obvious. Soybean, corn and hay fields stretch alongside any number of county roads, with farms often segmented only by a few rows of trees.

There is very little evidence of Native Americans in the region, although this was one of the last locations of the Eel River band, a subtribe of the Miami Nation, before most of them were forced from the state in 1846. Many of the Eel River people were born, lived and were buried in Boone County, yet so little was captured of their lives and so little proof exists today.

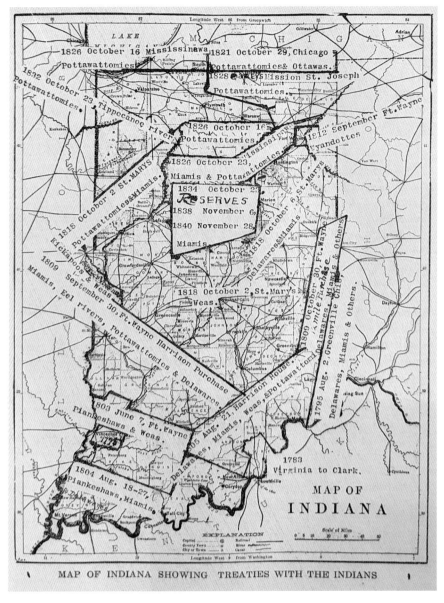

Map of treaties with the Native people of Indiana. *From* The History of Boone County *by L.M. Crist, 1914.*

The Miami Nation has many other subtribes, such as the Wea, Piankashaw and Mengakonkia. The lands they inhabited for centuries would eventually become the states of Michigan, Wisconsin, Illinois, Ohio and Indiana. By the mid-eighteenth century, the majority of the Miami Nation were living in central Indiana, after being pushed into the state by the Iroquois. Many settled at the convergence of the Eel and Wabash Rivers alongside the Potawatomi Nation for several decades.

The Eel River band received their name from this Indiana river location. The river's name, Kineepikwameekwa Siipiiwi in the modern Miami spelling system, came from the abundance of American eels found in the river at the time.

This land in northern and central Indiana was ideal for farming several varieties of corn, a crop that was sacred to the Eel River band's lifestyle. While corn was a primary staple of their diet, they also planted melons, squash and pumpkins and collected berries from the forest. Each year they held a festival in the fall to celebrate the harvest and another in the winter to acknowledge the return from hunting grounds with meat, furs and maple sugar.

The Eel River band lived peacefully on the banks of these rivers until an increasing number of colonists began moving west, urged by the new nation selling land to pay its war debt. When a group of Kentucky militiamen destroyed the village of one Eel River band in 1791, it's presumed they relocated to the banks of Sugar Creek near the present area of Boone County's Thorntown.

Around this same time, the government began to establish treaties with Native Americans, both to limit warfare and create boundaries in order to sell the land to settlers. The first treaty that impacted the native peoples of Indiana was one that included land from Western Ohio into Indiana. The Treaty of Greenville was signed on August 3, 1795, in Greenville, Ohio, with Miami chief Little Turtle representing multiple nations and signing on their behalf. The treaty established what was then called the Old Indian Boundary Line, ceding enormous tracts of land in the Midwest to the United States government. This section started from the mouth of the Blue River in Kentucky, then headed north to Fort Recovery, Ohio. The treaty gave Native Americans all land west of the Old Indian Boundary Line, with the exception of a six-square-mile tract where Fort Wayne currently exists, a six-square-mile tract near Fort Ouiatenon in Indiana and other smaller tracts in various sections of the state. This treaty forced more members of the Eel River band into Indiana from Ohio, along with a large portion of the Miami Nation.

THE TREATIES

From 1795 until 1809, at least seven different treaties impacting the Miami and other Native people were drawn, bit by bit encroaching on the land, forcing them to move elsewhere. Shawnee, Delaware and Miami Nations met in various negotiations and ceded the land that they believed they didn't need. These treaties began to put Native Americans at odds with one another as some Nations agreed to these treaties, while others weren't consulted.

Older chiefs like Little Turtle attempted to maintain the peace and abide by the terms of these previous agreements, while younger tribe members were dissatisfied. The Shawnee chief Tecumseh claimed that these treaties weren't binding because all native groups hadn't agreed to them.

Little Turtle's influence began to wane at the same time Tecumseh's influence began to rise. William Henry Harrison, as governor of the Indiana Territory, was tasked with acquiring land from the Native Americans for white settlement. In 1809 he penned the Treaty of Fort Wayne, which ceded nearly 3 million acres by the Miami, Potawatomi, Delaware and Eel River people. For Tecumseh, this was the last straw. He

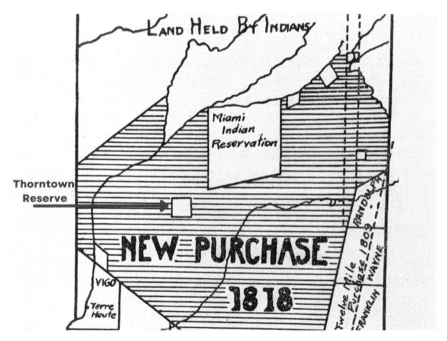

The Treaty of St. Mary's created an island of reserved land in central Indiana for the Eel River band. Land surrounding the Thorntown Reserve was quickly sold to an influx of settlers. *From* The History of Boone County *by I.M. Crist, 1914.*

and his followers demanded the treaty be nullified and the land returned, including a portion located in Boone County.

A series of conferences held in Vincennes came to no conclusion. The War of 1812 temporarily paused the discussion and any new treaties. Some Native Americans sided with the British, while others, including the Miami, sided with the United States. Little Turtle's death in 1812 could have pushed Tecumseh's agenda further, but the Shawnee chief died in 1813 at the end of the war, dissolving his goal of a tribal confederacy.

The Treaty of Saint Mary's in 1818 had one of the most significant impacts on future settlements in Indiana. Six separate treaties were established between the U.S. government and the Ottawa, Wyandot, Potawatomi, Wea and Delaware. These treaties gave virtually all of central Indiana to the government. The treaty signed last, with the Miami Nation, ceded land north of Raccoon Creek and opened the way for future Boone County land to be sold. The Treaty of Saint Mary's officially established six reservations for the Miami, one of which filled the entire northwest quarter of Boone County. Many members of the Eel River band had been living on this land for decades, but the treaty officially gave them one hundred square miles or roughly 64,000 acres. This included 54,400 acres in present-day Boone County and 9,600 acres in bordering Clinton County.

THORNTOWN'S ORIGINS

The Eel River people had named the primary village Kaawiahkionki, or "At the Thorns." Eventually the community established in this spot was simply called Thorntown. It was positioned at the center of the reservation, roughly five miles in each direction to the border. Although much of the southern part of the county was swamp, the northern tract was ideal for farming. The land was irrigated by the Sugar Creek River, or Ahsenaamiši Siipiiwi. This became the first permanent establishment in the county and the first acknowledged evidence of a Native American presence. While no verified presence of other nations has been discovered, the Delaware and Kickapoo were known to live nearby and possibly would have hunted or set winter camp in Boone County.

The first known permanent French trading post was established in the 1790s at Kaawiahkionki, likely when the band moved from the Eel and Miami Rivers. French immigrant Peter (Pierre) L'Anglois moved to the area from

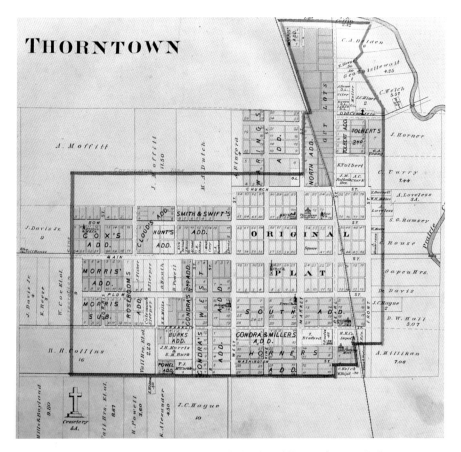

Map of Thorntown, circa 1878. *From* Historical Atlas of Boone County, Indiana, *Kingman Brothers.*

nearby Tippecanoe County. He was one of the few non-indigenous people licensed to live and trade in the area, bartering beads, blankets, powder and guns for furs. L'Anglois married a Miami woman named To-pe-naw-koung. Some of their children traveled with them as they ventured from state to state, while others, who had grown, were also traders and given sections of land for trading posts through the Treaty of Saint Mary's. Although L'Anglois wasn't granted a license until 1824, his land was deeded in 1818, and settlers reported meeting him in the area in the early nineteenth century.

By 1800 two important trails crossed in Kaawiahkionki. The Fort Wayne Trace stretched from Vincennes in the southwestern part of the state all the way to Fort Wayne in the northeast. The Great Trail began to the east in Fort Greenville, Ohio, running all the way to Fort Dearborn in Chicago.

A section of this trail connected Kaawiahkionki to a group of Delaware along Indiana's White River. Their village, Strawtown, was roughly thirty-five miles to the east, along the former trail now known as Strawtown Road. Another trail led from Kaawiahkionki to Terre Haute. It's difficult to say whether any trails existed before 1800 or whether they were created to connect to other communities after the area was established, but many of these trails eventually became routes traversed by wagons and cars.

While the Treaty of St. Mary's provided a reservation to the Eel River band, it also encouraged the surrounding land to be sold, including the remainder of Boone County. By the early 1820s, new settlers began building homes in this uncharted area.

EVICTION

Approximately four hundred members of the Eel River band lived peacefully among the newly arriving settlers in Boone County for a decade, until landholders began to recognize that the Thorntown land was one of the more valuable and easily farmed sections of the county. The Eel River leaders were drawn into a treaty in 1828 that was the beginning of the end for Kaawiahkionki. The Eel River band ceded their land and gave up their reserve at a treaty made at the Wyandot Village in Tippecanoe County on February 11, 1828. It was established between the United States government and the "chiefs, headmen and warriors of the Eel River, or Thorntown Party of Miami Indians," as they were identified in the treaty.

The agreement gave the Native Americans until October to vacate the land and move to a smaller reservation near Logansport in nearby Cass County. This land, located along the banks of the Eel River, was the same area where some had lived a generation earlier and where they would rejoin Miami from other areas of the state. In leaving Thorntown, they were instructed not to burn or destroy any current homes and told that they would receive a total sum of $10,000 in goods for sixty-four thousand acres. The government promised to build twelve log homes and clear and fence forty acres of the new land. Peter L'Anglois was promised $1,000 in silver and $3,000 in goods. The treaty was ratified May 7, 1828. Once the band was in Logansport, President John Quincy Adams ensured that they received all promised provisions from the treaty except one. He withheld $5,000 that was to be used for education of the Eel River and Miami children.

Soon after the Eel River band moved from the county, the land was available for sale at the Federal Land Office in Crawfordsville. Reserve sales of the sixty-four thousand acres opened on November 10, 1829, with the land selling for $1.25 to $4.00 per acre. Within a few months, every bit of Boone County land had been sold. However, the forced eviction wasn't the end of the Eel River band in the county. While most vacated the reservation, a handful managed to stay, refusing to be pushed away. They were initially greeted with trepidation by the new landowners.

As for those evicted to Logansport in 1828, they lost their land yet again in 1840 when a final treaty ceded all property in Indiana and Ohio in exchange for land on a Kansas reservation along the Osage River. Some individual members of the Miami Nation, including the families of Chief Richardsville, Frances Slocum, the Godfreys and Peter L'Anglois, were given tracts of Indiana land as part of the agreement. Some of their ancestors remain in the area today.

Those who weren't granted land were told to leave Indiana within five years. In 1846, when they hadn't yet left, the government threatened to withhold annuity payments. Near the end of that year, 328 Miami people boarded five canal boats to be transported out of the state. Although many who had been granted Indiana land in the treaty were exempt, some chose instead to join their relatives and friends rather than be ripped apart. The boats passed many former Miami villages and ancestral burying grounds on their way to an Ohio River steamship in Cincinnati. The final stretch to Kansas was taken by foot. Seven deaths were recorded on that journey.

In 1867 they were pushed once again into Oklahoma to live among the Osage and Quapaw people. Other tribes such as Ottawa, Shawnee and Wyandot had also been forced from the Midwest into Oklahoma, where they were able to remain. Today their descendants are collectively known as the Miami of Oklahoma, while relatives who remained are now recognized as the Miami Nation of Indians of the State of Indiana.

The Miami were among the last Native groups to live east of the Mississippi. Their removal marked a new era in America and a rush of settlers. By 1830, Boone County's census recorded 622 people, comprising approximately 125 families. That number didn't include those few Native Americans who remained; they were no longer recognized by the government.

THE EEL RIVER BAND TODAY

As Boone County grew, there was limited recognition of Native Americans who once called the land their home. The first settlers shared stories of interactions with the few who remained. These anecdotes referred to kindness and help offered by those Eel River people while the settlers were growing accustomed to the new land. On occasion, residents around Thorntown unearthed items such as arrowheads, pieces of pottery or beads. In 1914, skeletons presumed to be from the Eel River band were exhumed during construction of Thorntown's water mains. They had been buried with items such as a pipe, silver crosses and silver bracelets. The location of the bodies and the relics today remains a mystery.

It wasn't until 1972 that an effort was made to embrace this past. The Society for the Preservation of Our Indian Heritage was founded to explore and promote the county's Native American history. Within two years, the group had a membership of 275. They staged the first Festival of the Turning Leaves in 1973 to honor Native American culture, inviting those from the Miami Nation to celebrate their heritage with drumming and dancing. The event honored the Eel River band's traditional fall harvest festival. By 1998, the number of people interested in these traditions had begun to wane, and the expense of hosting the powwow became too great for the small community. Festival organizers opted instead to focus on education versus what was termed the community's "sad" history. The festival still continues as a three-day event with a parade and music to benefit the Thorntown Historical Society.

In 1993 descendants of the Oklahoma Miami Tribe desired to purchase a tract of land in Boone County as a federal trust. Their goal was to establish a cultural center and museum and to reestablish the Eel River heritage in the area that had been their home for so long before they were forced to Oklahoma. Initially there were concerns by Boone County residents that the property might be used as a casino, but tribal representatives assured the community that the property would be used to restore native heritage to the county.

For several months, Boone County commissioners heard arguments on both sides of consideration and in 1994 signed an agreement to donate 350 acres. The new facility, located next to the interstate, would also serve as an attraction for those traveling through the county, and the land would provide powwow grounds for native people. Both sides anxiously awaited approval from the Department of the Interior. On July 28, 1994, the application was rejected by the Bureau of Indian Affairs, stating that they believed gambling would take place even though the agreement expressly prohibited it.

The Oklahoma Eel River and Miami Tribe appealed the decision, and the following year their application was rejected again by the Department of the Interior, which stated that the location was too far from Oklahoma to be properly maintained by the tribe. The DOI believed that because Boone County was more than five hundred miles away, there would not be enough staff or resources to visit and manage the property uses.

No other requests have been made by Native Americans and the Miami Nation to obtain land in the area. As of 2021, while there are descendants of the Eel River band across the country, their official representation in Indiana has diminished.

Chapter 2

Beginnings of Boone

Indiana officially became a state in 1816, and by 1820 much of the land was available for purchase. While the Thorntown Reserve is considered the first part of the county to be inhabited, Eagle Township in the southeast corner of the county was next. The first people purchasing land in this area were David McCurdy and Ezekiel Rice, in 1822. Patrick Henry Sullivan was the third on record, yet he was the first to move to the county and create a farmstead. Sullivan along with John King, James and John McCord and Jacob Sheets were among these first intrepid settlers, but none of them took steps to incorporate their acreage into an official community.

The distinction of creating the first recorded town in the county was left to John Gibson. On October 3, 1828, Gibson purchased eighty acres of land along a heavily traversed road, dreaming that he could turn it into a viable stop for travelers. This route between the state's capital and the Federal Land Office in Crawfordsville seemed an opportune spot for food and lodging. He partnered with James Matlock to bring this dream to reality. The two men platted a sixteen-block town, with Matlock owning the eight blocks on the north side of the highway and Gibson owning the eight blocks on the south side. A coin toss decided who should name the town, which Matlock won; he immediately named it Jamestown. Locals are apt to feel themselves on a personal level with Matlock and call it "Jimtown."

When Jamestown registered in the Hendricks County courthouse on March 10, 1830, Boone County was a month shy of becoming an official

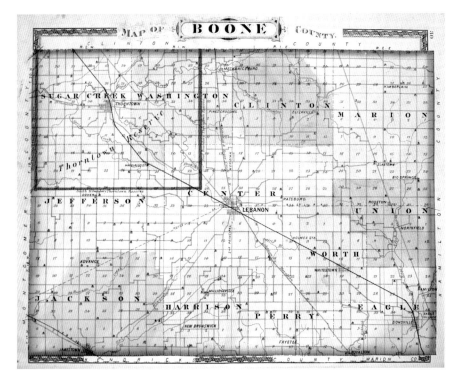

Map of Boone County, circa 1878. From *Historical Atlas of Boone County, Indiana,* Kingman Brothers.

entity. The Hendricks County office maintained management and judicial control over the paperwork because there was no other governing body at the time to do so. It wasn't until 1836 that the Indiana General Assembly decreed that the plat could be recorded in Boone County as if it had never previously been recorded elsewhere.

The county was established on April 1, 1830, but what to call it garnered some debate. Some in the Indiana General Assembly wished to name it Mercer County, while others vied for Ray County in honor of then-governor James Brown Ray, but the supporters of naming it in honor of Daniel Boone eventually won.

The county lines were drawn in a rectangular shape encompassing 420 square miles or 268,800 acres. From east to west it runs 24 miles, and from north to south it spans 17.5 miles. Originally eleven townships were created: Sugar Creek, Jefferson, Jackson, Washington, Clinton, Marion, Harrison, Perry, Eagle, Union and Center. Worth Township was added in 1851, pulling land from Center, Union, Perry and Eagle Townships.

Jamestown's Main Street before being paved. *From the collection of Harley Sheets.*

Why this was done is unclear; in 1856 fire destroyed the Boone County courthouse and along with it the official paperwork. One plausible reason is the railroad, as it was likely named for railroad secretary Alexander Worth. Whitestown was created the same year as the township, and both may have been created for tax purposes. Township lines were occasionally redrawn in the early years, as commissioners would grant any petition, whether it was for taxes or convenience.

The original plat for Thorntown was filed by Cornelius Westfall two weeks after the county officially came into being. The papers were filed at the Hendricks County Courthouse because a Boone County recorder or recording office had yet to be established. Westfall platted twelve blocks, reserving a public square at the northeast corner on which he hoped the county courthouse would sit. Because the area had already served as a town and seemed to be more inhabitable than the rest of the county, Westfall was optimistic that Thorntown would be selected as the county seat. He placed ads in the *Indianapolis Journal* on February 23, 1830, prior to registering the town, to sell the town lots:

> *The subscriber will offer at public sale on Thursday, the 15th of April next, a considerable number of lots in the town of THORNTOWN: Situated in Boone County, Indiana, thirty-five miles North West of Indianapolis;*

twenty-five miles South East of LaFayette; and twenty miles a little North and East from Crawfordsville. One third of the purchase money will be required in hand, one third in six months, and the balance in a year. The site for a town is not surpassed for beauty by any in the state, being elevated to the height of about fifty feet above the water of Sugar creek, which runs near the place. It is said to be a place notorious for health, having formerly been an Indian town—and is surrounded by a vast number of never failing springs of good water, and convenient to a constant running stream with good seats of mills, & c. It is also well situated for the intersection of several leading and important roads. Sale to commence at 10 o'clock.

Once Boone County was officially formed, a group of delegates from neighboring counties was tasked with appointing a county seat. By that time, Jamestown had a population of less than a dozen log houses but was far more inhabited than the rest of the county. Its relatively robust population led the delegates to choose this spot in the southwest corner as the seat of justice.

In a short time, there were complaints from other residents, numbering 622 by the end of 1830. A lack of roads made it difficult to reach Jamestown, so establishing a county seat in another far-reaching corner was unlikely,

Downtown Thorntown. *Courtesy of the Thorntown Heritage Museum.*

despite Westfall's hope that Thorntown would be the choice. To placate the dissenters, the state legislature passed an act requiring that the seat be relocated to a spot within two miles of the geographic center of the county.

Two Indiana militiamen had wagered this might happen. In 1830 General James Perry Drake and Colonel George L. Kinnard purchased land at the county's center and set about platting a town of nineteen blocks surrounding a public square. Kinnard, who happened to be the Marion County surveyor, had already ensured that a planned road from Indianapolis to Lafayette would take a slight jog through their anticipated town.

To sweeten the prospect with the Indiana state legislature, the two men donated every third lot in their original plat, plus a town square and forty more acres outside of the current town limits, back to the county should the county seat be placed there. By the middle of 1832, the governor appointed a delegation of five representatives to find the spot for the new county courthouse. Jamestown had held the county seat distinction for less than two years before it slipped away.

Finding a location in the middle of wilderness, however, wasn't going to be easy. The book *Early Life and Times in Boone County, Indiana*, written in 1887, refers to the location of Lebanon as being "a tall, dense forest of large trees, among which the small growth of underbrush and saplings were so dense as to obstruct the passage of man or beast."

The five men tasked with finding this spot were also required to give it a name. Adam Miller French from Montgomery County was the youngest of those tapped for the assignment. He returned to Lebanon in 1877, nearly fifty years after that day, to give a speech recounting his role in the location and name of Lebanon.

"How could it be done," he relayed. "In every direction for more than two miles the water seemed to almost cover the face of the earth, and the most gigantic forest ever mortal man beheld grew up out of the strong rich soil."

The five men debated whether the location should be along the projected Indianapolis-Lafayette Road or on the site of land donated specifically for county use. French cast the deciding vote in favor of selecting the donated land. Once they had settled on a location, a larger debate ensued, as the group couldn't agree on a name. French recalled his attitude: "I regarded it as only barely possible ever to make a town here," he said.

In frustration he lay down at the base of a tree to nap. The group soon awakened French, having decided to allow the oldest and youngest of the group to draw lots for the honor of selecting a name. French won the draw.

He admitted in his speech that he was tired and would have settled on the first name that came to him. Looking around, he saw the tall trees and told them that he was reminded of biblical stories read to him by his mother. He said that a straight-standing group of hickory trees reminded him of the Cedars of Lebanon, and therefore he suggested Lebanon as a name. He also recalled that a large group of bystanders—who were, oddly, watching the delegation make their decision—gave a cheer.

It was long rumored, even in his obituary, that French had another motive for the name. French was born in Lebanon, Ohio, and spent his childhood there. It's plausible that was the basis of his selection, instead of a biblical inspiration.

More than a dozen communities in Boone County were established over the next two decades, with many of them fading soon after the turn of the twentieth century and most gone a century later.

In 1830 the plan for Eagle Village began when William Miller purchased eighty acres in the southeast corner of Boone County and had it surveyed by Colonel George Kinnard, who founded Lebanon. The plat had eighteen blocks of 108 lots lying on both sides of a stagecoach route. Several months later his sons Thomas and John, along with their cousin James McCleland, set out to create the town. They made their way from eastern Indiana by wagon, ferry and canoe before reaching the home of David Hoover at the southeastern edge of Boone County. From there the men cut their way through thick underbrush to the location along the Michigan Road, under construction at that time. They quickly built a log structure for a dry goods store, which flourished when the road was completed later that year.

Royalton was next to be established, in 1832. It began as Rodmans, named for the postmaster William Rodman, who was an early inhabitant of the town. It's said that the name was changed because the village saloonkeeper sold whiskey by the "royal ton" to area settlers.

Clarkstown followed in 1833, named for Walter Clark. It was situated less than a mile north of Eagle Village, along the same stagecoach route. In 1834 Northfield was established another mile north. All of these towns began to disappear when the road was no longer in popular use.

Mechanicsburg, originally called Reeses Mills, was platted in 1835 by James Snow and is located north of Lebanon, near the junction of Sugar Creek and Brown's Wonder. Its first name was given by the general store's owner, Joseph Reese, who also served as postmaster. The name was soon changed when a gristmill was built, requiring many mechanics to aid in its construction.

Whitestown's Main Street around 1915. *From the collection of Harley Sheets.*

Several other towns were platted as the railroad established routes across the county. Stops like Max, Terhune and Hazelrigg Station were created to meet the need of a stop every eight to ten miles along the route. When the railroad ceased operations, these towns dwindled to only a small cluster of homes.

Three Boone County towns that were built with the railroad yet survived its departure are Zionsville, Whitestown and Advance. Zionsville began with David Hoover, who settled in the southeast corner of Boone County in 1824 with his wife, Rebecca, and their three children: Jacob, Isaac and Mary, better known as Polly. Their farm was the first to be located at the junction of Big Eagle and Little Eagle Creeks. Over time Hoover began to acquire surrounding land from early purchasers such as Patrick Sullivan. When Boone County was established in 1830, Hoover was elected to be clerk. He issued the first marriage license in the county to his daughter, then nineteen years old, and Elijah Cross in 1831. When Hoover died suddenly on Christmas in 1835, his daughter and new son-in-law inherited and purchased the entire Hoover property. Cross partnered with Lebanon businessman William Zion to create a new town through which the train would pass.

Whitestown was originally called New Germanstown when it was platted by Ambrose Neese in 1851 as land for the railroad was being graded. In 1853, when the community was unable to secure a post office with that

Main Street, Advance. *Courtesy of the SullivanMunce Cultural Center.*

name, it was renamed Whitestown, most likely for Congressman Albert S. White of Lafayette, who also served as president of the Lafayette & Indianapolis Railroad.

Advance became a town in 1872 when a new train route was proposed north of Jamestown. Jackson Township farmer William Stiles saw the route of the proposed new train and decided the adjacent land would make a good town. Stiles was a savvy businessman but illiterate. He bought eighty acres of land just south of the railroad crossing, signing his name with an *X*. The community was initially called Osceola, but when they tried to establish a post office, a town with the same name located in a nearby county necessitated a name change. Residents decided that getting a post office would "advance" the community forward and chose that name instead.

CHAPTER 3

THE STAGECOACH

Although much of central Indiana was waterlogged, very little was navigable. A series of canals like those that were operational in the northern part of the state could not be created further south. State leaders realized they needed a ground transportation plan so that settlers could connect with each other and the rest of the country. The legislature proposed more than two dozen roads in 1820, joining towns and extending to the interior. When the state capital was moved from Corydon in the southern corner of the state to a centralized spot, there was an accelerated demand for reliable roads in central Indiana. In 1826 the state proposed the Michigan Road to connect the northern and southern boundaries of the state via Indianapolis and the eastern edge of Boone County.

A good portion of the land to create this massive road was ceded by the Potawatomi Tribe to the United States by the Mississinewa Treaty of 1826. The federal government then donated the land to Indiana with the intent of creating a military route from the Ohio River to Lake Michigan. Surveying the road was underway in 1828, but it wasn't until 1834 that the entire length of 264 miles was finished at a cost of about $240,000. That expense was paid by the sale of one section of land contiguous to each mile of the road. The portion of road that would run through Eagle Village was cleared by 1829, creating an initial passage—albeit a rough trek—between Indianapolis and the land just north of Boone County.

The Michigan Road was between eighty and one hundred feet wide, with a minimum of thirty feet flanking each side. That area was reserved to pile the lumber cut from the dense forest. The road itself varied between twenty and thirty-five feet wide. The roots of the trees were so deep that a special process was enacted to uproot them. Zionsville resident James Dye recalled the process in 1902. "The trees were grubbed out by the roots, many of them being four feet in diameter. A huge log was dragged in a position that would allow the grubbed tree to fall on it in such a way that the root end would be lifted out of the hold and then hauled to one side and cut into logs and hauled off the center of the road," he said. Dye added that any rain created such a slush, horses could find themselves neck-deep in the mud. But they had no other options, because there was no other road. Cut trees left by the side of the road created a tunnel of trunks, with no access in or out until the wagons came upon the next opening. Thousands of dollars of valuable wood were simply left to rot. Many pioneers later lamented the waste.

Once the trees were removed, the road was graded, the holes were filled, and bridges were built over streams. Eagle Village was officially platted in 1831, and by the end of that year, the road was completed and ready for four-horse carriages carrying mail and passengers. The average cost for the stagecoach was five cents each day, traveling at an average rate of sixty miles per day.

Newspaper editors estimated that the Michigan Road was the second most popular route in the country, second only to the National Road, which was the first federally funded interstate connecting the country from east to west, starting in Cumberland, Maryland, and traversing along the Potomac and Ohio Rivers to Illinois.

Several inns and taverns were popular stops in towns that today are only marked by a simple sign along Michigan Road. The Larimore Tavern in Eagle Village was one of the most frequently visited. Jacob Jones' Inn in Northfield was another alternative for those who wished to travel a mile or two further.

By 1835 at least two-thirds of the state was accessible by highways. Several ran through Boone County, quickly boosting new towns that appeared on the route. By then the Indianapolis-Crawfordsville Road had been in place for roughly a decade. With Jamestown located roughly midway on the route, hotels, taverns and livery stables capitalized on the traffic. Coaches left Indianapolis three days a week, heading to Crawfordsville, where riders could continue onward to Chicago, Wisconsin or Michigan.

In 1829 the Lafayette State Road was graded and cleared, connecting Thorntown to the north and south. This road, which would eventually become U.S. Route 52, was surveyed by Colonel George Kinnard. Upon discovering the road's nearness to the center of the county, he slightly shifted

Built in 1832, the Larimore Tavern was a popular stop for stagecoaches along the Michigan Road before it was destroyed in the 1920s. *Courtesy of the SullivanMunce Cultural Center.*

the route to run through the center and then purchased the land that would eventually become Lebanon.

In the early days of these roads, weather dictated whether the trip would be short or painfully long. As a *Zionsville Times Sentinel* editor recalled in 1903, when weather was dry, "a hundred teams could be seen at one view" along the Michigan Road. Yet rain made the roads nearly impassable. "It was a common thing to see a stage, pulled by four horses get stuck in the mud, and not only did the passengers have to get out of the coach, but often each one of them had to carry a rail to pry the coach out of the mud," the editor reported.

Many solutions were attempted to make travel more predictable. Jamestown installed corduroy roads on Main Street. Logs were laid side by side to support the wagons and prevent them from sinking into the earth. This wasn't always successful; the log sometimes sank into the mud, or those that weren't well stabilized sometimes floated away during significant downpours.

Roads were often the butt of jokes. Zionsville resident Nathanial Swaim joked that in the 1840s in Boone County, "we had roads in those days, but you had to get down to the bottom to find them."

The south side of Lebanon's courthouse square. *Courtesy of the Boone County Historical Society.*

Some roads were plank roads, with flat milled boards laid on the ground, creating a wooden floor over the earth, and fastened with spikes. Often toll roads used this method because the ride was easier and could be traversed much more quickly. This was good in theory, but over time, planks were known to sink into the earth or float away with rain. The wood itself generally lasted fewer than ten years. By 1859, Indiana enacted a law that tolls could not be collected on roads not being kept in good condition and that plank roads were no longer allowed. By then gravel had become the material of choice.

There were several techniques using gravel in Indiana. One, devised by John MacAdam, became known as a macadamized technique. This surface began with crushed granite in a shallow trough, which was covered with smaller, lighter stones so that water would run into drainage ditches on either side of the road. The technique was later improved with the Telford-Macadam system, which utilized various-sized stones from largest on the bottom to smallest on top. The stones were compacted together, forming a road that could withstand more wear and tear. The process was expensive and thus was only used on those frequently traveled routes in the county. The rest remained dirt.

Tolls were collected on two gravel roads within Boone County, one on the Michigan Road by Rosston and the other between Thorntown and Darlington in Montgomery County. Taxpayers living along these roads purchased them and, in 1884, turned them over to the county to be maintained as part of a free gravel road system.

Other county roads and wagon paths emerged from existing Native American trails and trading routes, several of which converged in Thorntown. Thomas P. Miller reported following one such trail on a trek from Eagle Creek to Lafayette around 1832. At the time there were no other communities between the southeast and northwest corners of the county. He said that he and his traveling companions didn't encounter another soul for twenty-four miles, not until they reached Thorntown.

CHAPTER 4
THE RAILROAD

In 1847 the first intercity railroad arrived in Indianapolis from southern Indiana. Railroads had been proposed in the state since 1832, but the effort didn't gain any traction until the middle of the century. Soon plans for multiple routes were proposed, including the Lafayette & Indianapolis Railroad, which planned to pass through the center of Boone County.

Lebanon resident William Zion was appointed as a special commissioner to the project. One of his tasks was to create stops approximately every ten miles along the seventy-three-mile route. In Boone County, he planned for stations in Thorntown and Lebanon, with Eagle Village reportedly planned as the southernmost stop. It's likely that Zion leaned upon a director of the L&I Railroad to create a station between Lebanon and Thorntown. Major Harvey Hazelrigg donated tracts of his land to create Hazelrigg Station, and a small community was born. At roughly the same time, Whitestown was created, approximately ten miles southeast of Lebanon.

The proposed railroad track was straight, except for a single curve after it entered Boone County's southeast corner. Constructing the railroad over flat, straight land kept costs low and productivity high. In 1851, grading was complete from Lafayette to Lebanon, while five-sixths of the grading was completed between Lebanon and Indianapolis. The bridge over Eagle Creek was the last portion to be finished. Sometime between the first railroad discussion and 1851, plans to utilize Eagle Village seemed to deteriorate. Fifty years later, George Reveal recalled in the Zionsville newspaper that Eagle Village residents were asked to provide an incentive to bring the

Whitestown's train station, around 1914. *From the collection of Harley Sheets.*

railroad through their community. Residents "would have none of it," and instead the tracks shifted to the west. Perhaps that is the entire story, perhaps Zion wanted to avoid a portion of the track running through Hamilton County for tax purposes or perhaps he never intended to connect to Eagle Village. Regardless of the reason, by 1851 Zion collaborated with Elijah and Polly Cross to use their land in the southeast section of the county for a new train station. They platted a town of six full blocks, three half blocks, and five quarter blocks. The Crosses donated land for the railroad, a school and a church, finalizing their work in November. The paperwork was filed on January 26, 1852.

Elijah wanted to name the town Marysville, to honor his wife and the land she had inherited. She declined and the two men decided to name it Zion's Village. After a very short time, the name was changed to Zionsville. The Cross's granddaughter, Rebecca Gates, would later recount, "Mr. Zion named the town but Mr. Cross gave the land."

By 1851 tracks were laid from Lafayette to Lebanon. Passengers completed their journey to Indianapolis via stagecoach until the route was finished a year later. The Lafayette & Indianapolis Railroad eventually became the Indianapolis, Cincinnati & Lafayette Railroad and then became known as the Big Four for the cities it connected: Cleveland, Cincinnati, Chicago and St. Louis. When it changed hands again in 1930,

An early photo of Zionsville's depot from tintype. *Courtesy of the SullivanMunce Cultural Center.*

Polly Cross donated land with her husband, Elijah, to start the village of Zionsville. *Courtesy of SullivanMunce Cultural Center.*

it was purely for freight transport. The railroad between Zionsville and Lebanon was discontinued in 1976, and the stretch between Lafayette and Lebanon halted in 1985.

While the railroads were used to transport travelers, half of their use was for freight such as hogs, corn and wheat. Eagle Village and Jamestown, once heavily reliant upon stagecoach travelers, began to suffer. Residents of Eagle Village moved their businesses and homes to Zionsville, but those in Jamestown had to wait patiently for their own rail system. A route was planned in the late 1850s; then the Civil War halted any possibility of progression. It wasn't until 1868 that the Indianapolis, Bloomington & Western Railroad considered expanding their line with a stop in Jamestown. The rail was completed the following year, and Jamestown began to thrive once again. The track eventually was known as the Cleveland, Cincinnati, Chicago and St. Louis and then the New York Central railroad before being

Lebanon's Big Four Depot. *From the collection of Harley Sheets.*

purchased by CSX. It's one of two active tracks in Boone County, once used by Amtrak but now only used for freight.

In 1882, the town of Terhune was established in the northeast corner as the only Boone County stop along the Chicago, Indianapolis and Louisville Railroad. It would eventually be known as the Monon Railroad. A small town known as Kimberlin, or Possum Trot, was located a mile south, but many inhabitants moved to Terhune to be closer to the rail.

In 1875 the Anderson, Lebanon & St. Louis railroad began its charter with plans to run between those cities. Within a few short years, the company went bankrupt and reorganized as the Cleveland, Indiana & St. Louis Railway, which became known as the Midland Railway. It wasn't until 1887 that plans for the train to run through Boone County came to fruition. Advance and Rosston, founded in 1872 and 1874 respectively, were already on the route, but three other towns were created in its wake. Max, Gadsden and Heath were other stops along the Midland track, though the towns didn't expand much beyond a cluster of homes and an occasional store. That brought the train to eight of Boone County's twelve townships.

The last railroad to be built in the county was constructed in 1913, when the Pennsylvania Railroad made plans to connect several other lines for an alternative option from Indianapolis to Chicago. Because of its late construction, the route through Boone County only stopped at Lebanon and operated on elevated tracks through the city.

Trains were responsible for a large number of deaths, whether trains hit buggies or people passing too near the tracks. In 1906 Zionsville took action against trains speeding through town, enacting a resolution restricting them to fifteen miles per hour. That reduced the number of accidents but didn't prevent them completely. By 1921, since there was no longer a railroad stop in town, the tracks were moved several blocks to the west, where they remained until they were abandoned.

Chapter 5

The Interurban

Trains made travel easier between Boone County and the rest of the United States, but fifty years later the Interurban made travel easier within the county itself. First known as the electric train, it was soon called the Interurban, a mode of transportation between two cities versus travel within the same city. The term was coined by former Indiana legislator Charles Henry and was soon being used to describe these systems throughout the Midwest. Promoters boasted that riders could travel in the lap of luxury for a fraction of the price of a locomotive and in a fraction of the time.

The Interurban's entry into Boone County wasn't a smooth path. In February 1901, the Indianapolis & Lebanon Traction Company was incorporated with plans to create a route between those two cities and then extend to Lafayette. Among the board of directors from Lebanon were William DeVol and future governor Samuel Ralston. The company considered two possible paths: through Traders Point and Royalton or through Zionsville and Whitestown. The latter towns were selected by offering stock subscriptions and a significant subsidy, plus it appeared that particular route would be more popular, based on local ticket sales of the existing railroad.

As the Indianapolis & Lebanon moved forward, requesting right of way from individual parcels of land, another group of investors incorporated the Lafayette & Indianapolis Rapid Transit Railway to complete a route between those cities. Among those at the helm was James Zion, son of William, who

Jamestown's Interurban station around 1910. *From the collection of Harley Sheets.*

had planned the railroad in Boone County. The company intended to run parallel to the railroad for part of the route, then filed 105 eminent domain suits for additional right of way.

In short order, these two organizations were at odds, in particular for the land between Lebanon and Zionsville. They each filed a long list of legal complaints against one another, including a consideration that one group had tampered with a survey. Within a year, the Indianapolis & Lebanon had been reorganized to the Indianapolis & Northwestern Traction Company. They soon won the legal battle against the Lafayette & Indianapolis, which dissolved.

The I&NW was the largest Interurban undertaking in the state at that time, with more than $1 million in construction contracts. Townsend, Reed & Company was enlisted to develop financing and construct the line. Their recently constructed line from Indianapolis to Shelbyville had proven successful, and so Boone County leaders were invited to see firsthand how these trains operated. They reported to their communities that the ride had been smooth, fast and luxurious.

The I&NW completed their track through Zionsville, Whitestown, Lebanon and Mechanicsburg on October 11, 1903. Yet it wasn't the end of their struggles. They had plans to build a route from Lebanon

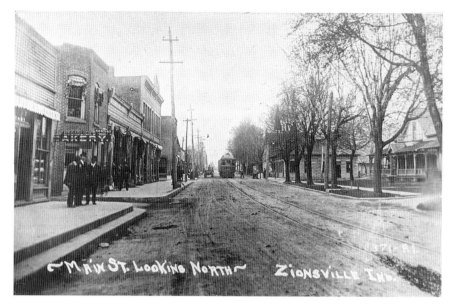

Zionsville's Interurban tracks ran the length of Main Street. Sidewalks had recently been installed, but streets were still dirt. *From the collection of Debbie and Greg McGrath.*

to Crawfordsville but encountered more problems when the town of Crawfordsville refused to grant access within the city. They found themselves in a battle with Consolidated Traction Company for sole rights to enter downtown. Citizens signed a petition to grant the right to I&NW; the town eventually concurred, and trains were able to operate by the end of 1903. These interurbans held fifty-two people and reached up to sixty miles per hour, versus the starting maximum of fifteen miles per hour for trains in 1852.

In Jamestown the possibility of the Interurban began to become a reality in 1905, when promoters of the Consolidated Traction Company reorganized as the Indianapolis, Crawfordsville & Western Traction Company. Passengers would travel directly from Indianapolis to Crawfordsville via Jamestown. Construction began in 1905, which included a depot at the corner of Mill and High Streets. Trains began running in 1907 with the "Ben Hur Special"—so named for Crawfordsville native General Lew Wallace, who wrote the novel—stopping in Jamestown hourly. Both the IC&W and the I&NW would be purchased by the Terre Haute, Indianapolis & Eastern Traction company, making it the second largest traction company in the state. Not only did it provide transportation, but it also furnished electrical power to cities in rural areas.

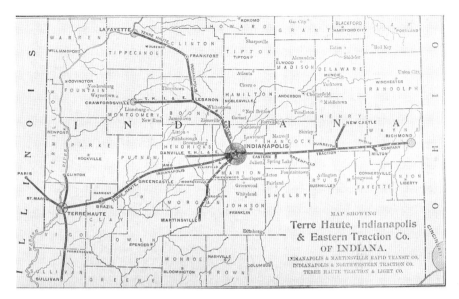

The Terre Haute, Indianapolis & Eastern Traction Company connected much of central Indiana. *From the* Commercial and Financial Chronicle, *1911.*

This left Thorntown without Interurban access. Robert P. Woods, hired as the civil engineer on the I&NW, recognized a need to connect the northwestern corner of the county and initiated a line specifically between Lebanon and Thorntown. The Lebanon-Thorntown Traction Company consisted primarily of local investors. The route was less than ten miles long, one of the shortest routes in the state. It was completed within a year of incorporation on July 4, 1905. The independent line had eleven stops, including Hazelrigg Station. Only two cars were in operation, known as "Dorothy" and "Frances," each named after daughters of prominent officers on the project. While the small enterprise was able to cover operating expenses, it never paid dividends to its investors. On August 27, 1926, when the Interurban's riders diminished, the trains stopped, and lines were sold to a scrap dealer.

By 1930 the THI&E was bankrupt. The last day of operation was October 30, 1930. The line and the rolling stock were dismantled. By then automobiles and highways had become the next phase in transportation.

Chapter 6

The Rise of the Automobile

The first reported automobile in the county was seen in September 1899. A "horseless carriage" stopped by the barn of Zionsville banker W.H. Alford for a few hours so that residents could gawk at the strange new mode of transportation. Many had seen an occasional vehicle in Indianapolis, but none had the opportunity to closely examine it. The spectators came and went all afternoon, with nearly everyone in the town seeing the car up close by the end of the day.

It wasn't long before automobiles were spotted along country roads, startling horses and causing many accidents. In one early instance, a newspaper reported that a buggy was smashed and the horse lighted for home, while the automobile "went serenely on its way as if nothing had happened." In another instance, two cars attempted to ford a flooded creek. They were stuck and, ironically, had to be pulled out by horses.

In 1900, a "locomobile" was sighted in Lebanon, driven by H.L. Kramer of Attica during a nearly two-hundred-mile trip through central Indiana. It was noted in the Lebanon newspaper that they traveled an astonishing thirty-five miles in two and three-quarter hours. The locomobile was run by steam generated by a gasoline fire. By the next year, two automobile owners in the county were at odds over who was officially the first. Cyrus Beamer of Zionsville and Fred Hoffman of Lebanon purchased their vehicles within a short time of one another and jested through their respective newspapers about who had the better machine.

Harry Kramer from Attica drove his 1900 locomobile through Lebanon, the first automobile on the city's streets. *Courtesy of the* Lebanon Reporter.

The introduction of the automobile created chaos in towns that had trains along one street and interurbans along the next. Horses that had grown accustomed to the previous forms of transportation would balk at cars chugging along the dirt streets. Wagons, trains, horses and automobiles all converged within a few blocks, many times resulting in tragedy.

The impassable roads did little to help. In September 1911 the last bricks were laid on Zionsville's streets so that mud would no longer be a factor. Brick was laid on the streets of Jamestown and Lebanon as well, providing some relief. Bricks were readily available and provided a more stable option than corduroy roads for those with automobiles. In some cases, such as roads in Advance, coal was poured between the felled logs in the street for a more level surface.

In 1915, transcontinental highway routes were being proposed by promoters for automobiles to move in all directions across the United States. Over the next several years, three of these routes were planned through Boone County, with Lebanon being the center. Two were planned to run north and south, and the third would run east and west.

Bricks were laid on many downtown streets, including Lebanon's, for ease of travel. *From the collection of Harley Sheets.*

Some of these highways were originally routes from Indianapolis. The Lafayette State Road, constructed to link that city with the capitol, once passed through Lebanon and Thorntown. By 1919, State Road 6 was created, running from Indianapolis to Lebanon, then turning north to Frankfort. Some highways like this one drove straight through Boone County fields, disrupting operations and making it challenging to farm. Joseph Coons was one farmer who took part in a four-person lawsuit when he discovered that the new highway would run between his home and barn. He lost the case, and the road was built.

By the turn of the century, maintenance of the Michigan Road had lapsed, leaving much of it impassable. When the Interurban stopped and automobiles and buses were the primary methods of transportation, the county was further hurt by the lack of options for reaching its communities. In 1931 the Michigan Road Association was able to get the road repaved, but by then farmers living along the road had encroached on the property, building fences and even some structures causing the road to be narrow along certain areas.

PART II.

PRESERVED PAST

CHAPTER 7

LEBANON'S COURTHOUSE AND DISTRICT

T he first settlers to arrive in Lebanon were somehow able to see through the thick trees, swamp and mosquitoes with a vision. It took half a century, but eventually the center of town, and thus the center of the county, became a hub of activity radiating out to the other communities. Some of the county's history is preserved and recognized by the National Register of Historic Places. Each of the Boone County sites on the list provides a different insight into the county's past. Some are private farmsteads and homes; others are rural districts. Some convey farm life through the Depression; others showcase dozens of samples of twentieth-century architecture. Some, like Scotland Bridge, are on the brink of fading away. Others, like the county courthouse square, are finding a renewed life.

The initial attempt to build a courthouse in Lebanon resulted in a small two-story log structure erected in 1833 on the north side of the square, a year after Lebanon was selected as the county seat. The second courthouse was built in 1839 at the center of the town square, with brick architecture resembling the original statehouse in Corydon, Indiana. Its stone foundation wasn't particularly steady or well constructed and eventually collapsed, rendering the building unsafe.

In 1856 a more substantial structure was planned, with a design that was initially popular among residents. The architect was renowned for designing the Christ Church Cathedral on Indianapolis's Monument Circle and Center Hall at Wabash College. Several decades later, however, residents' tastes had changed. They publicly grumbled about the design and wanted something

Boone County Courthouse. *Author's photo.*

with a different style. The gothic building was demolished in 1909, and a cornerstone for a new courthouse, the fourth one, was laid on November 30. The approved plan was for a neoclassical building to be constructed of Indiana limestone and granite.

The highlight of the design was the inclusion of eight monolithic limestone columns—announced as the world's tallest made of a single piece of stone—standing sentry at the north and south entrances. The stone pillars were quarried in 1910 at Stinesville, Indiana. The long columns arrived by train in octagonal pieces so they could be transported on a flat side. They were delivered to Lebanon via the Big Four Railroad on flatbed cars. Witnesses reported that three trucks of heavy planks were laid end to end along the street, then an upright stationary steam engine carried the columns to their final resting place in a painstaking process. As the mule-driven engine progressed forward along the planks, those planks that had been passed would be moved to the front and the engine repositioned to follow the wooden tracks. Six weeks after their arrival, the columns were rounded and smoothed with a final height of thirty-five feet. The massive columns, estimated to weigh thirty tons each, are still among the largest in the world.

Lebanon's third courthouse experienced three fires within a year. *Courtesy of the SullivanMunce Cultural Center.*

The interior of the courthouse has retained much of its original charm. The stained-glass dome, the second largest in the state, reaches four stories, blanketing the rotunda. The floors are primarily ceramic tile, and the wainscoting of the corridors and rotunda is white Italian marble with a green Vermont marble base. The rotunda floor marks the spot where Boone County and the courthouse are both perfectly bisected along the Second Principal Meridian line. The courthouse was constructed with brick walls and concrete floors, ensuring that it would be fireproof. County leaders had learned their lesson after the previous building experienced three fires within one year.

The courthouse was completed in late 1911 and was opened to the public on January 1, 1912. A huge celebration to dedicate the building took place on July 4, 1912, overseen by former vice president Charles Fairbanks. So many people from the Zionsville area rode the Interurban to partake in the festivities that it was the busiest day in the line's history. The streets were packed, and stores experienced record-breaking sales, yet a head count was

The massive columns on the county courthouse were the largest in the world when they were completed in 1911. *Courtesy of the Boone County Historical Society.*

A pushmobile race was part of the festivities to celebrate the county's new courthouse.
Courtesy of SullivanMunce Cultural Center, originally from Dorothy Stephenson Smith.

beyond reach. The *Lebanon Reporter* simply stated, "No accurate estimates can be placed on the size of the throng."

Over the following decades, the courthouse received updates and renovations, but its largest overhaul came in 1990, when the entire courthouse underwent a restoration. Skylights that had been covered were restored, and details like brass ceiling lights were given a new shine.

Although the courthouse was placed on the register in 1986, the surrounding district wasn't added until thirty years later and includes forty-eight properties. These include a Carnegie library, post office, jail, former high school, two churches and several two-story commercial buildings. Many of these buildings still bear the names of the builders, like "Hoffman Building," "Cowan" or "Cragun Block." Others are marked with "Bank" or "Reporter Building," identifying the building's use.

CHAPTER 8

CASTLE HALL

Zionsville's former town hall, located in the midst of its downtown, was built half a block off present-day Main Street. The two-story rectangular structure was dedicated in 1902 and only came into existence after a bit of controversy. For several years, residents had been clamoring for a public meeting location, while business owners simultaneously asked the town to construct sidewalks along downtown's dirt streets. How to fund these projects was the biggest debate.

In 1901 when the town was electing new trustees, three of the men running banded together to make a public commitment. J.J. Knox, H. McDaniel, and Milton Hussey promised that if elected, they wouldn't spend town money on a town hall, nor would they force property owners to construct sidewalks. The election came down to those who wished to use taxable funds to pay for these improvements versus those who wished to find other means. In a narrowly decided vote, the latter won.

The three newly elected trustees were immediately approached by business owners petitioning to allow them to construct sidewalks with funds borrowed from the town. The request was approved.

In a short time, the trustees were faced with a demanding public asking for a town hall and community center, citing the need for a larger meeting location as the town continued to grow. In early 1902, soon after the newly elected trustees took office, Zionsville's newspaper editor pressed the idea, saying the town "needs it, people want it, if somebody else will build it."

Zionsville's streets around 1900, before sidewalks were introduced. Mr. Hill, John Hussey and Milton Hussey stand in front of a local store. *Courtesy of the SullivanMunce Cultural Center.*

The trustees coordinated with the Knights of Pythias, a men's society of which the three were members, to help with the building if they could find land. A petition signed by 114 residents, including Milton Hussey, requested borrowing $7,500 to purchase real estate.

Only six months earlier, two lots had been purchased by a number of business owners, with the intent of creating a stable and hitching post, which was sorely needed as certain businesses didn't care to erect a hitching post in front of their establishment. Instead the designated property went to the new town hall. Whether the lots were purchased from those business owners or donated is unknown, but by spring of 1902 construction of the town hall building was rapidly underway at the address known today as 65 East Cedar Street.

The structure was dubbed Castle Hall, in part because of its association with the Knights of Pythias. The Knights of Pythias was organized in 1864 as a secret society to promote social and humanitarian causes. Their buildings were generally constructed to have the appearance of medieval castles. Another Knights of Pythias structure also known as Castle Hall was built in 1894 in Lebanon. That building still stands today, although its original three stories were shortened to two after a fire in 1944. The Knights of Pythias, a national organization, was active in many Boone County communities, including Thorntown and Jamestown, and some groups are still engaged in the county.

Zionsville's Castle Hall was constructed to serve not only as a town hall, but as a multipurpose community center. The town planned to retain the first floor for government offices and a public auditorium, while the Knights of Pythias would utilize the second floor as their lodge, promising to also maintain the roof.

More than two hundred thousand bricks were used in construction, sorted to be of uniform color in the front. Castle Hall held a lodge room, banquet hall, small meeting rooms and auditorium. The building was heated by furnace, and more than one hundred gaslights were installed in the building to illuminate the meeting rooms and stage.

While the initial cost was expected to be $2,500, the final cost was nearly double, with $1,500 going toward bricks. Part of the expense likely was the detail to the interior of the building. Parquet flooring, ornate woodwork and pressed metal ceilings in three different patterns still exist in the building's entryways. Downstairs a side door once led to public lavatories. The Knights of Pythias's emblematic crest was said to be embedded in the wallpaper upstairs.

The downstairs portion was extremely popular. Within a year, rooms in the building were rented to theater groups; Columbia Vaudeville Company, Zionsville Dramatic Club and Goldy Wade's Imperial Lady Minstrels all performed there.

The building's completion sparked interest in two other government-based structures. Nearby, Whitestown's trustees proposed establishing the community's first town hall but received backlash from residents who didn't want to face an increase in taxes. The story was different in Lebanon, with a new courthouse being approved and constructed within the decade.

The first year after it opened, Zionsville's town hall hosted a wide variety of events, such as wrestling matches, concerts, plays, an oyster supper and a violin solo. Over time it served as an occasional skating rink, basketball gymnasium and dance hall. Graduation ceremonies, minstrel shows and community performances were held there. Even though the auditorium seated 488, more than once it was packed beyond capacity, with chairs placed in the aisles and people standing around the perimeter.

In 1922 and 1923, it served as a temporary school. Seventh and eighth grade classes were held on the second floor while a new school was being

Zionsville's Castle Hall. *Author's photo.*

constructed. One teacher recalled having to clean out the stovepipe from the coal stove several times per week and remembered that soot would permeate the classroom.

In 1923 the building was the site of a fall fair. An Indianapolis newspaper reported that it was complete with "exhibits of cattle, hogs, fruit, vegetables and a hundred and one other things, all contributed by folks within a six mile radius of Zionsville."

Every Wednesday and Saturday night in 1912, a film was shown on the building's second floor. By 1924 two movie theater enthusiasts signed an agreement with the town to allow films to be shown more frequently. Windows on two sides were filled with bricks to darken the room.

In 1935 former movie theater owner Clyde Harris signed an agreement to rent the hall and continue the movie operations. Seven years later he purchased the building from the town, added improvements and turned it into a full-time theater. Harris died suddenly in 1945, and his widow and daughter took over the operation.

In 1963 the former town hall and movie theater was converted into the Zionsville Village Playhouse for community shows. It didn't last long. The theater troupe moved to less expensive accommodations elsewhere, and the building was converted to shops and offices.

Today the building is privately owned and divided into offices, services and private apartments. Some windows are still filled with bricks, and very little is left of the grand interior that was once the pride of the town.

CHAPTER 9

ULEN HISTORIC DISTRICT

The town of Ulen began as a country club, then evolved five years later into a community of homes that are recognized as being uniquely distinctive in their architectural styles. Although Ulen is its own incorporated community with its own town board, it's completely surrounded by Lebanon. Many of the fifty-three homes in the small neighborhood are adjacent to an eighteen-hole golf course and country club, all created thanks to the support of one prominent citizen.

Henry C. Ulen grew up in Lebanon in the 1870s and '80s. He was often described as being a restless child and spent more time getting himself into trouble than learning. After leaving Lebanon schools at the age of fourteen, he held a wide variety of jobs for short periods of time. He was a newspaper correspondent, worked county fair concessions, was a telegraph operator for the Central Indiana Railroad, worked in a dining car and at one point was deputy postmaster. Although he never completed high school, he studied law and passed the bar exam in 1894.

In 1899 he created the American Light & Water Company to install municipal utilities in Indianapolis. Within ten years he had moved to Chicago and soon became a banker. By 1916 he started the Ulen Contracting Company; their first assignment was to complete water systems in several cities in Uruguay. He was able to fund the project with bonds, opening opportunities for similar projects in Europe and the Middle East. In 1921 he contracted with the Bolivian government to build a railroad system throughout the country. Simultaneously he was in the midst of constructing the Shandaken Tunnel, at that time the longest tunnel in the world, to provide drinking water to New York City through a gravity-propelled system. The eighteen-mile-long tunnel still provides residents with water today.

Through the years the company planned, financed and constructed systems such as railroads, tunnels, sewer systems, hydroelectric developments and irrigation projects around the world. One large project that still stands today is the Marathon Dam in Athens, noted for using native marble to blend the dam into its historic surroundings.

Ulen continued to connect with friends back in Lebanon and expressed interest in starting a golf club in the town. He promised to fund the course if they could find land near the city. A site was found, but the estimated cost at the new location was double the original proposal. Ulen approved it, and in 1923 construction for the Ulen Country Club began. He purchased land north and east of the club with the thought of either expanding or creating a small community.

As Ulen's career was booming, he decided to move his company's headquarters to Lebanon. In order to accomplish that, he needed his employees to have a unique neighborhood filled with high-end homes worthy of moving from New York City. In 1929 he established the township of Ulen on forty acres next to the golf course, partly as an incentive for his top employees. Eight officers along with other prominent citizens of Lebanon built impressive homes, while Ulen built his own Mediterranean-style mansion so that it would be only steps away from the country club.

To ensure the builders could continue to progress during winter months, Ulen had his home enclosed in a box at a cost of roughly $10,000. The home itself spared no expense: leaded glass windows, hand-scraped oak floors, an owl carved into the newel post and a carved marble fireplace. The home was unveiled with a champagne bottle broken on the box to celebrate the removal of the surrounding shell.

By the time the Great Depression hit, the company was recognized by an Indiana magazine as being "the largest engineering and contracting corporation in the world." The company continued projects and kept the Ulen Country Club operating into World War II. After the war there were plenty of other contractors, and Ulen's business slowly faded away.

When the town was established, Ulen ensured that utilities would be buried; thus there are no power lines above. It's one of the first communities in the world to do this, certainly utilizing the experience that Ulen Contracting Company had with infrastructure. Today the home styles vary from Tudor to Colonial Revival and from Mediterranean to

Ulen's home was enclosed in a box and unveiled when construction was complete. *Courtesy of the* Lebanon Reporter.

Ranch. It incorporates nearly every popular home style within a span of fifty years from the early to mid-twentieth century.

The country club has its own historical significance. The two-story red brick building retains its original floor plan, with an enclosed veranda, ballroom and original clay tile roof. A mural of the golf course wraps around the walls of the dining room. The basement once housed a bowling alley. As the only country club in Boone County, Ulen Country Club has been the site of social, political and cultural gatherings in the community for nearly a century.

The course itself remains the same as when it was redesigned from nine to eighteen holes in 1927, after Ulen donated forty-three additional acres. Very few other historic courses have maintained their original plan. The course, with century-old trees, was designed by William "Bill" Diddel, who spent his final years in Zionsville. This was the first of more than three hundred courses designed by Diddel in thirteen states.

Chapter 10

Howard School

On an acre of land in Perry Township, tucked between farmland and an old cemetery, sits the last unaltered one-room schoolhouse in Boone County.

The Howard School's existence is a rarity that could have had a very different future. Similar one-room schoolhouses were converted into homes or sheds. Some now house farm animals. Many others were demolished.

The one-room schoolhouse was once ubiquitous. In 1910 there were 9,300 schoolhouses in the state, of which 123 were in Boone County. Then, in 1910, Indiana began the first of many steps to consolidate rural and township schools. By creating a smaller number of centralized schools, the state would save money on teachers, maintain fewer buildings, provide more programming for students and ensure healthy facilities at a minimal increased expense for transportation. The initial plan was to create one school per township.

By 1920 the number of one-room schoolhouses in the state had dropped to 4,500. Over the next several decades, larger schools were constructed in many towns and townships, and the small schoolhouses lay empty and deserted across the state.

In 1982 an inventory of historic sites showed that twenty-nine of the county's schoolhouses still existed in various stages of decay. By 2004 twelve from that inventory no longer existed. Another five had been converted to large buildings with a variety of uses, eight had been converted to private homes, one had become a barn and another had become storage for farm

The Howard School was presented with a bell from another Boone County schoolhouse, now gone. *Photo by Mara Lusk.*

machinery. Of the two remaining, one was in significant disrepair, housing farm equipment. The other became the Howard School.

John Howard was one of the early settlers in Boone County, purchasing eighty acres in Perry Township in 1837. He became the township's first trustee, and it's likely that's why he agreed to have a school built on his property around 1855. The original wooden structures were rebuilt every few decades, until a brick schoolhouse was erected in 1881. That school was colloquially known as the Howard School but was officially called Perry School #1. It was the first of six total schools to serve students in the township. During the 1916 Christmas vacation, the Howard School and the five other schools closed to make way for a new, larger school in Perry Township to start the new year.

The Howard land was transferred from owner to owner over the decades. In 2004 owners and siblings Kenneth Washburn and Kay Seymour offered to donate the brick schoolhouse and their property surrounding it, if someone was interested in restoring the building. Their plan was to demolish it if they couldn't pique any interest. By then the building had been sitting idle for nearly a century.

Township resident Jack Belcher was intrigued. He rallied friends for a meeting to see who might be up to the task. A core group of seven people were convinced to join Belcher on one condition: when it was complete, they didn't want to be in debt. They quickly established tax-exempt status through the newly organized Howard School Restoration Group. Their efforts resulted in many private donations, as well as grants from groups such as the Boone County Rural Electric Membership Corporation and the Boone County Community Foundation.

The group's first glimpse of the schoolhouse was discouraging. A tree was growing in the middle of the building, the windows and floor were missing, the roof was unsalvageable and plaster from walls had crumbled, exposing the lathe beneath. Despite all those issues, a structural engineer deemed the foundation to be solid. The foundation was so solid that it didn't move years later when a truck backed into it.

Inside the building, very little was salvageable. The group was able to find some inkwells and a patch of original floor by the door, but nothing else was left intact. Volunteers collected materials from similar-era buildings, including the dilapidated schoolhouse that was being used to store farm equipment. That building was near collapse, so they negotiated the use of its bricks to be used for repairs at the Howard School. With plenty of bricks

A tree was growing inside the old school building before renovation began. *Courtesy of the Howard School Board of Directors.*

The Howard School during restoration. *Courtesy of the Howard School Board of Directors.*

remaining, they built a walkway and restroom, as the original school had utilized an outhouse for its students.

To save money, the group relied on their own skills whenever possible to restore the property. They searched for guidance online when they didn't know how to complete certain tasks, such as replacing the shake-shingle roof. The hip roof has a flat deck at the top center, the arched windows use white mortar between the bricks and the arched openings are reminiscent of Italianate architecture, which was very popular in Indiana in the 1880s. Window openings were originally a four-over-four double-hung sash. Each window had a limestone sill with an arched header.

Over time they fitted the interior with desks, slate blackboards and two hitching posts outside to recreate what students in grades one through eight would have experienced. A school bell, previously used at Union Township School #1, was donated by the Boone County Historical Society. The floor was replaced with material that matches the original flooring, which was discovered in one corner and remains intact.

It took seven years of sweat, tears and perhaps a little blood. The restored building was dedicated on May 1, 2011. Among those at the dedication was Hazel Tharp, who had been a student at the school when it unexpectedly closed during Christmas break in 1916. Tharp, born in

1903, was instrumental in answering questions about the school's interior and exterior as the Howard School Restoration Group attempted to recreate the furnishings.

Rather than convert to the official name of the school, the intrepid volunteers who brought the school back to life believed that honor and recognition of John Howard should live on.

The Howard School is available for field trips for adults and children. Volunteer schoolmarms teach students for an hour or a day. Students learn math, health and spelling interspersed with recess and lunch at the Howard School's remote location, 4555 East 750 South.

The Howard School Restoration Group continues to raise funds to cover annual expenses such as lights, maintenance and insurance for the building. They sell engraved walkway bricks, host chili dinners and hold a yard sale each year at the school, with all of the proceeds used to maintain the property.

Chapter 11

MAPLELAWN

Maplelawn could just as easily have been erased and turned into a community park. Instead it was added to the National Register of Historic Places for its encapsulated perspective of life on an Indiana farm during the Depression. The Zionsville farmstead's sixteen historic structures built between 1850 and 1945 show the progression of farming over one hundred years.

The farmstead began in 1835 when John and Jane Wolf purchased their eighty-acre property in Eagle Township, clearing enough land to plant corn and build a simple home. Once the railroad came to Zionsville just a few miles away, their farm began to prosper. Many farmers had the same experience, finding it easier to reach a large number of buyers for their crops as transportation expanded. In particular, Boone County was known for exporting wheat, corn, hogs and cattle.

It seems the current Maplelawn house was built during this time of prosperity, likely around 1860. It was built in the form of an I-house, so named because many versions were located in *I* states like Iowa, Illinois or Indiana, although they can be found almost anywhere across the country. An I-house generally has two stories, two rooms equal in size on each floor and a gable in the center.

Like many historic properties, the home's original shape has spread and evolved over more than a century. It has elements of Queen Anne spindles, with a Craftsman porch supported by brick squared piers. The back of the house stretches to incorporate two former outbuildings, one used as a

Maplelawn farmstead. *Author's photo.*

milk room and the other as a shed. They were most likely connected to the main structure after the turn of the century, when the kitchen breakfast nook was added.

In the 1870s, after Jane Wolf died, John deeded the farm to two of his daughters, Eliza Wolf and Nancy Klinger, splitting the property. After John passed away, both parcels were sold in 1900 to Elroy and Elmira Scott, uniting the land once again. Thus began a century of the Scott family's ownership of Maplelawn. The Scotts seem to have been the first to give the farm its name, due to the large number of maple trees around the homestead.

Between 1900 and 1925, manufacturing industries blossomed in the state. Iron, automobiles and machinery began to boom as agriculture began to suffer. Boone County lost almost 30 percent of farmland to industrialization, more than double the average amount in the state. Despite this, Maplelawn continued to grow. The family added a barn, a chicken coop and hog houses.

When the Depression hit, chickens and dairy were the two mainstays on the property. Other nearby farms suffered, and farmers lost their land, but Maplelawn persevered.

Elroy died in 1942, and his son Merle passed away soon afterward. In 1945 the estate left the property to Alyce Bradley, the granddaughter of Elroy and Elmira Scott and only child of Merle Scott. Alyce and her husband, Lester, decided to continue operation of the farm, growing wheat, corn and soybeans. They converted one structure to a dairy barn and sold hogs and sheep. The couple farmed together, with his and hers tractors and his and hers combines. In the 1960s they added a machine shed and round metal grain bin.

Alyce passed away in 1997. Lester donated thirty-seven acres of their homestead across the street from the house to the United Methodist Church in memory of his wife, so the church could construct a new building. He continued to farm approximately five hundred acres of the original property, and in his leisure time he would hunt and fish with longtime friends like Eddie Shortz and Donald Spees.

When Lester passed away, the town purchased his property, intending to raze the farm buildings and turn the land into a community park. Concerned residents formed a committee to save four acres of the property with the fifteen farmstead structures. They proposed establishing a nonprofit organization in order to lease the land from the Zionsville Parks Department for fifty years. The town accepted the idea, allowing Maplelawn Farmstead Inc. to become reality and turning the remainder of the land into Mulberry Park.

The farmstead organization actively keeps the work of its predecessors alive by hosting architectural and farm camps for students, movie nights and mystery dinners. They encourage projects from FFA, Scouts and 4-H. Maplelawn's gardens exist as they would have during the Depression, with an herb garden, vegetable garden, berry bushes and several patches for flowers.

CHAPTER 12

PRYOR BROCK FARMSTEAD

As Maplelawn is an example of a farmstead with a popular I-style home, the Pryor Brock Farmstead is a farm property with an equally popular Italianate style in both its home and outbuildings.

The Brock family moved to Indiana in 1829 and to Boone County a few years later, on a farm eight miles east of Lebanon. In 1846, twenty-three-year-old Pryor Brock married Emeline Stoneking. They became members of Salem Methodist Episcopal Church in the Traders Point Hunt Rural District. It wasn't until 1861 that they purchased land for farming. In 1865 they bought the parcel on which they would place their home that stands today. At one point Brock owned nearly 260 acres, a notable accomplishment when roughly three-quarters of farmers in the county had less than 100 acres.

The Brocks built a new home in 1870 to reflect their success in farming. The Italianate two-story house was built on a foundation of enormous field stones, possibly left from glaciers. Molding, brackets and scrollwork decorate the trim. The home has four bedrooms on its second floor and maintains much of its original woodwork inside. Over time the house absorbed several detached outbuildings, such as the summer kitchen and springhouse.

In the early years of the farm, the Brocks built a basement barn with a large portion of the foundation nestled into the edge of an embankment. The barn housed livestock, and with advances in technology, it was eventually used to store modern farm equipment. By 1910 a drive-through granary was added, with sliding wooden doors. The center alley allowed

The Pryor Brock farmstead. *Author's photo.*

vehicles to easily access the dried grains, an efficient method of transporting and selling them. Additional outbuildings that are still standing include a privy and a workshop.

By the turn of the century, the Brocks had also planted a great number of sycamore and maple trees. The property still contains some of these century-old trees.

When Pryor and Emeline built their house, many of their ten children were grown. They were prosperous farmers for the time, producing far more corn and wheat than other farms in the county. They also raised hogs and chickens, but grains were their primary staple.

Emeline Brock died in 1884. Pryor remarried but passed away in 1898 at seventy-five. Their farmstead was split among heirs but remained in the family until 2006. Today the farmstead has been reduced to nearly five acres and is privately owned.

Chapter 13

The Simpson-Breedlove House

Were it not for a concerned bulldozer operator, the Simpson-Breedlove house might only be a memory today. Instead the home's planned destruction was brought to the attention of the SullivanMunce Cultural Center in Zionsville, which worked with Indiana Landmarks to find a way to rescue it.

The house was initially built by Marcus (Mark) Simpson. Simpson was born in Ohio and moved to Boone County in 1852, where he first worked as an attorney and later cofounded Farmer's Bank in Zionsville. He married Caroline Duzan in 1863, and they settled in Whitestown briefly before moving to a large property along the Michigan Road. At the time, it's surmised that there was a log cabin on the property, but within short order the couple built a beautiful two-story brick home. The design is considered transitional; the low-pitched roof, tall windows and dental work indicates an Italianate style, then elements of Greek Revival were incorporated with straight lintels over windows and stone sills. The first story originally had a parlor, sitting room, library and kitchen, while the upstairs had three bedrooms. The home had three chimneys and a staircase with two curves.

Shortly after Simpson built the home, Caroline suddenly died. Simpson decided to sell his newly built home to John McKenzie Breedlove, who was also born in Ohio. Breedlove grew up on a farm and sold his land in Ohio to pursue farming in Indiana with his new wife, Mary Ellen Cox. He bought the house from Simpson and, over several decades, purchased surrounding land until his property expanded to more than eight hundred acres. It's assumed he farmed some of the land himself and rented the rest to stock farmers. When Breedlove died in 1909, his sons rented the home and farm to the Essex family until 1938. A member of the Essex family who lived in the house as a young boy later recalled that seed corn was stored in one of the home's bedrooms.

In the 1940s Breedlove's descendants sold the property and home to Frederick Holliday. Holliday also rented it, first as a complete home and then segmented into multiple units. The land continued to be farmed by renters, and the home was occupied until 1982, when the upkeep proved to be too much. Holliday boarded the home, and it sat empty for more than ten years. In 1994, Holliday decided to raze the brick house to create more farmland. That's when the bulldozer operator intervened, reaching out to the local historical museum. Indiana Landmarks convinced Holliday to donate the home so that they could find someone willing to restore it, with the covenant that the exterior maintain its current form.

It took some time to find the right buyers, but in 1996 the home was purchased by Gary Essary and Jerry Hamm. After decades of neglect, it needed significant work; it had no heating or electricity, and a section of

The transitional style of the Simpson-Breedlove home. *Photo by Sara Baldwin.*

floorboards had completely collapsed. The impressive staircase, however, was in excellent condition and was the feature that convinced them to take the plunge.

Over two years, they restored the home to its former glory and improved on it by providing insulation, expanding the electricity and updating the kitchen. They also added a foundation, as the home had been built on rubble stone and hadn't been reinforced for more than one hundred years. Hamm and Essary did much of the work themselves, including electrical, woodworking and flooring; they also relied on family for additional assistance. More than half of the windowpanes contained the original glass, and they stripped many layers of paint from window frames and doors.

Eventually they added a barn, which served as a garage and woodworking shop. They also created a kitchen garden and summer kitchen, both of which had been part of the early homestead. The couple planted new trees and added an herb garden.

In 2018 Hamm and Essary were approached by developer Steve Henke, who had purchased the farmland from Holliday and wanted to incorporate the home into his six-hundred-acre housing development and golf course. Reaching retirement age, Hamm and Essary were ready to sell. The home will eventually be incorporated into retail shops designed to blend in with the historic home. The developers plan to additionally add fencing around nearby Cox Cemetery, which houses the graves of soldiers from the War of 1812.

CHAPTER 14

OAK HILL CEMETERY

Traversing the paths of Oak Hill Cemetery is like traversing through history. Nineteenth-century headstones mingle with markers from the twentieth century, then the cemetery blends into twenty-first-century grounds with easily maintained plaques embedded into the earth.

Graves located near the original entrance were placed in the late nineteenth century. These family plots include markers in all shapes and sizes. Further along the drive, graves are more uniform in size and lower to the ground. This lawn-park style was encouraged in cemeteries when ease of maintenance was recognized as an important factor. By the 1950s, Oak Hill Cemetery moved toward a memorial park design, treating each grave equally regardless of importance. Markers are located level to the ground in neat rows, making lawn maintenance simple.

The oldest gravestones' Victorian-era carvings make them works of art, filled with meaning behind the headstones. Graves are marked with a variety of symbols, such as books, tree stumps, drapery and anchors. The many symbols indicated belief in God, marriage, youth or sorrow. Others feature a memorialized design. Samuel S. Doyle's monument of a solider firing a rifle is an exact replica of the memorial of the Chickamauga Battlefield near Chattanooga, Tennessee.

A massive thirty-foot column from Chicago's City Hall and Cook County Building marks the Neal family plot. As a business leader and organizer of the Oak Hill Cemetery, Charles Freemont Stephen Neal had the Virginia red granite column erected to mark the family's location near the cemetery's

An intricate carving in Oak Hill Cemetery marks several graves. The column marking the Neal family plot is visible in the background. *Author's photo.*

signature oak trees. His father, Judge Stephen Neal, is buried nearby in a plot marked by a granite column topped with a bronze bust of his likeness. As a contemporary of Abraham Lincoln, Judge Neal is credited with writing the first four of the five sections of the Fourteenth Amendment, granting equal rights to all persons born in the United States. Most of Lebanon's noted former residents can be found here: Henry Charles Ulen, Harvey Hazelrigg, Strange Cragun, Indiana governor Samuel Ralston and dozens of veterans from the Civil War.

Some graves at the entrance were installed within the past fifty years, but the road leads to a knoll with a circle of the signature oak trees where many of these notable residents were laid to rest. Foot and vehicle paths wind through the center of the cemetery, following its history. The Midland Railway, which became the Central Indiana Railway, once passed adjacent to the cemetery; today a trail has been created where train tracks once lay.

Oak Hill's history began in 1872 when the town recognized there was no more room in its unnamed publicly established cemetery, eventually known as Cedar Hill Cemetery. Samuel Rodefer purchased just over nine acres of land east of the city to be established as a new cemetery and named it for himself. The first burial occurred two weeks later when five-year-old Fannie Earhart accidentally fell backward into a tub of boiling water, fatally scalding herself. Over the next year, seventy-eight people were buried there, of which fifty-one were exhumed from Cedar Hill and reburied in Rodefer Cemetery.

Rodefer sold the lots for fifteen to twenty dollars each, with a reduced price for two or more lots. Each lot had enough space for six graves. Over time it was shown that Rodefer didn't tend the property well. Frustrated and concerned citizens founded a group in 1899 with the intent to purchase the land from him and establish a board of volunteers to maintain the property. They chose the name "Oak Hill Cemetery Association" due to a wide-spreading white oak tree growing on the grounds. The association still maintains control of the property, managing day-to-day operations and acquiring additional land for expansion over the years. Today the 115-acre cemetery has more than sixteen thousand grave sites, a chapel, a limestone office building and an English-style barn used for maintenance storage. Less than half of the cemetery property is filled.

Oak Hill Cemetery has two entrances: one opens into the oldest part of the cemetery, and the second has a grander presentation. The Washington Street entrance is quietly flanked by cobblestone columns and a small iron gate. The road leads past a limestone office building and curves past the town's original graves, with a circular drive centered with oak trees. In 1904

The limestone arch for Oak Hill Cemetery is one of two entrances. *Author's photo.*

the Lebanon Federation of Women's Clubs raised money for a Main Street entrance leading through a massive limestone arch to greet visitors. The road leads directly to the Powell Chapel, built in 1930 as a memorial to the Knights of Pythias and the Improved Order of Red Men.

The chapel is itself a historic site, designed by Lebanon resident R.J. Pfeiffer. The Gothic-style church includes a bell tower with buttresses at each corner. Walls are constructed of Indiana limestone as well as pink granite. Windows are filled with original amber glass. The chapel faced structural damage over the past two decades and is currently unusable. Efforts to raise funds to preserve and restore it were unsuccessful, and it is slated to soon be demolished.

CHAPTER 15

THORNTOWN'S LIBRARY

In 1908, Thorntown residents were in the midst of trying desperately to find someone to donate a library, something that the community lacked. A minister hoped returning native Anson Mills would be the answer, as he had planned to make a community contribution. Instead Mills elected to update the town's water and sewer system, so the idea for a library had to wait.

In 1912 the town got a temporary library when school superintendent Frank Long made the book collection in his office available to the public. The 425 books were significant, but the location was not an ideal long-term solution. Long soon applied to the Carnegie Corporation to help fund something more permanent.

Philanthropist Andrew Carnegie was well known for encouraging the growth and expansion of libraries in communities across the country. Between 1886 and 1919, Carnegie would help fund 1,689 buildings at an expense of more than $60 million. The majority of these, an estimated 70 percent, were in small towns, and they are located in every state except Alaska, Delaware and Rhode Island.

The original request from Long for a donation of $6,000 was increased to $10,000 when Sugar Creek Township joined the effort and agreed to help with the annual maintenance. In 1914 Carnegie agreed to donate the $10,000 to build a library if the town would provide a suitable site and agree to pay $1,000 annually for operating expenses.

Thorntown's Carnegie library is one of nearly one hundred still operating as libraries in Indiana today. *Author's photo.*

Carnegie's generosity was helped in part by limiting architecture and design expenses. Towns were allowed to select from six layout templates; therefore today many of these Carnegie libraries have a similar appearance. The templates even recommended a back side that was flat to accommodate future growth.

The Thorntown library was built with a basement for events, high windows to accommodate shelves around the interior walls and an open first floor that could be subdivided as needed. The brown brick exterior was completed with a hipped roof and limestone trim. Construction was completed in early 1915. It served as the library for the school system until a new school with its own library was built in 1955.

Today nearly half of Carnegie's libraries are still in use as public libraries, including two in Boone County. Lebanon's own library is recognized as part of the Lebanon Historic District. Indiana boasted more Carnegie libraries than any other state with 164, of which twenty have been demolished; two-thirds of those remaining are still operating as libraries.

Chapter 16

The Rural Historic Districts

Two contiguous sections of Boone County celebrate the rural history of the area. The Traders Point Hunt and Eagle Creek Rural Historic Districts together comprise more than 2,200 acres of land selected to represent particular landscape features such as waterways, vistas and pastures. These features are virtually unchanged since the area was founded approximately two hundred years ago.

The Traders Point Eagle Creek Rural Historic District and the Traders Point Hunt Rural Historic District vary in their scope and primary use. While the district surrounding Eagle Creek is primarily agricultural farmland and homesteads, the smaller Traders Point Hunt district was used for recreation and equestrian activity, along with its agricultural and community use. The two are the state's only rural historic districts adjacent to a metropolitan area.

The vast majority of the Traders Point Eagle Creek Rural Historic District lies outside of Boone County. Just a small portion extends from Marion County, where the bulk of the designated area lies, overlapping into Boone County along Eagle Creek. The district is bordered to the north by I-865, then ends just south of 79th Street. The west side is roughly bordered by Cooper Road, and it follows Eagle Creek on the east. Not only were the homes, farms and landscape significant, but Moore Road also dates to 1830, maintaining its same location and configuration today.

The Traders Point name harkens back to a trading post in the early nineteenth century and the town that was established there along Lafayette

The Traders Point Hunt was the oldest accredited foxhunting association in Indiana until it ended in 2018. *Courtesy of the SullivanMunce Cultural Center.*

Road, just south of Boone County. The surrounding land was used for livestock and dairy farming, country estates and equestrian activities. The Traders Point Hunt Rural Historic District was known as a rural getaway for the movers and shakers of Indianapolis. The Fortune, Krannert and Lily families were among those who owned property used for leisure activities. This spot at the southern edge of Boone County was less than a day's ride from the large city, making it perfect for vacation homes and recreation. The current district comprises approximately five hundred acres of land, containing barns, houses, bridges, a recreational camp, two cemeteries and the Queen Anne–style Salem Methodist Church. In all, fifty-nine structures, buildings and sites are part of the district. They range from English-style barns and silos to Greek Revival architectural homes and early twentieth-century bungalows. Wild Air and Bit Whip Farms, with their individually fenced pastures, are currently intact, presenting equestrian life and the hunt.

The most significant activity in the area for eighty-four years was the Traders Point Hunt, which ended in 2018. For many decades it was the oldest accredited foxhunting association in Indiana. The hunt was a drag hunt, versus a live hunt, meaning a scent was dragged through the hunting area for dogs to track versus tracking a live animal. The land that includes the Traders Point Clubhouse and course has a gambrel-roofed horse barn, the hunt kennels and a 1920s farmhouse.

The boundaries of the district are primarily defined by the contiguous farms that have contributed to the area and are associated with the Traders Point Hunt. The farms all collectively worked together so that riders could pass from farm to farm for long rides. The area is well recognized for equine activities but also for architecture, farmland, streams and bridges. The district doesn't comprise just a few items but a variety of unique pieces interconnected to form a unique hamlet in Boone County.

CHAPTER 17

THE STRANGE CRAGUN HOUSE

One of Lebanon's oldest homes still standing is known as the Strange Cragun home, built in 1893. "Strange" doesn't refer to anything unusual about the house but instead the unusual name of the home's builder.

Strange Nathaniel Cragun was born in 1857 in Eagle Township in Boone County. He was one of nine children, some with unique names, such as Melvina, Nebuchadnezzar and Columbus. There are two theories for the origin of Strange's name. The initial presumption was that he was named after a minister, possibly a circuit rider. Recently the family of Strange's brother Nebuchadnezzar reported that Strange had one blue eye and one brown eye and thus received his birth name.

Strange attended school locally and finished a year at Purdue before an appointment to the U.S. Military Academy. Regardless of the color, his eyesight was poor enough to have him removed from the military academy after two years. He returned to Boone County and served as principal in Whitestown, Zionsville and Lebanon schools.

Strange and his wife, Adelaide (Booher), moved to Lebanon in 1883 and soon inhabited a modest home a few blocks from the courthouse at the edge of town. Several years later Cragun applied his educator skills to run for county superintendent, a position he held until 1891. Once his elected term had ended, Cragun purchased the *Lebanon Patriot*, the county's oldest continually operating newspaper at the time. As his paper was Republican in focus, he had a friendly editorial war with Ben McKee, who owned the competing Democrat-focused newspaper, the *Lebanon Pioneer*.

Two years later the Craguns built a massive Queen Anne–style home to the front of their property at 404 West Main Street, maintaining both houses on the lot for several years. Gaslights were installed in the home, but knowing that electricity was coming, Strange planned ahead for an easy conversion; thus the home's fixtures can be used either way. The house was originally heated by steam from a boiler plant downtown. When the plant closed, the house converted to coal and eventually to gas heat. Doors in nearly every downstairs room open to a wraparound porch that extends along the entire front of the house. The home was once surrounded by mature trees, and windows to the east and west would be opened to further cool the house in the warm summers. The home's original clapboard siding is still intact. Wide and shallow steps lead to the front door, a massive oversized piece with a beveled glass window. A corner tower, balcony with balustrade and gables atop the second and third stories evoke the late Queen Anne style.

Before construction began on their new home, the Craguns welcomed twins Opal and Ethel in 1885. Tragically Opal died of scarlet fever near midnight on Halloween at the young age of six. It struck so quickly that she attended school the previous day, and her fever didn't worsen until half a day before she died. Ethel died at the age of eleven and was buried on Easter Sunday. Doctors thought she contracted scarlet fever from her sister more

The Strange Cragun House in Lebanon. *Author's photo.*

than five years earlier and carried the symptoms until her death. Although Opal passed away before the Cragun house was completed, the twins' matching furniture came to the new home.

Son Dwight was born a month before Opal's death. His time as a brother was too brief; he became an only child after Ethel's demise, and it was well known that his many aunts doted on the young boy. The Cragun parents traveled the world while Dwight stayed home with his unmarried aunts. Many travels were for business purposes, while others were recreational. Strange sold the newspaper in 1913 and became director of the First National Bank for twenty-five years. In 1916 the governor commissioned him to be a member of the State Tax Board, during which time he amended Indiana's tax law.

After his parents passed away, the house transferred to Dwight, who lived there with his wife, Mabel, and their four children. The home never left the Cragun family. Once Dwight and then Mabel died, the house sat vacant for about a year before being gifted to the Boone County Historical Society in 1988. A part of the gift was the home's considerable contents, including three generations of family acquisitions. The home itself was a veritable time capsule. Inside the historical society discovered dozens of family quilts along with vintage clothing, original furniture, traveling trunks and china. Punch bowls, silver, books, Native American items and original appliances were also left in the home along with boxes of receipts and bills for corsets, groceries, wallpaper, the piano, coal and travel. Nearly nothing, it seems, was discarded.

Most of the home has been restored to resemble the early years when Adelaide and Strange inhabited it. Many pieces found in the home are on display. Travel cases lie open in the bedrooms, ready to be filled with exquisite clothing for the next trip. Original hand-carved furniture in the parlor is adorned with decorations, such as fish or feet on crystal balls. The family's original Bible sits by the window, listing events in beautiful script. A massive 1900s-era mirror rests in the dining room, with built-in cabinets overflowing with family china. Each of the three fireplaces are unique, with different tiles and carvings on oak mantels. Pocket doors separating many of the downstairs rooms remain intact. A single stained-glass window is positioned midway up the second-story stairs.

When the house was restored, the historical society noticed intricate wood on the pocket doors but little to no gingerbread trim in the rooms. Mabel evidently hated dusting and had the trim removed, but it was discovered in the attic, and the historical society was able to match the nail holes to those still existing in the walls.

Today the home is available for events, tours and meetings.

CHAPTER 18

THE COUNTY'S ROUND BARN

O ne of Boone County's private buildings on the National Register of Historic Places is the Van Nuys Round Barn.

Round barns are a familiar feature in Indiana. The state once touted itself as the "Round Barn Capitol of the World," with good reason. Indiana had an official count of 226 round and polygonal barns built between 1874 and 1936, totaling more than any other state. Some researchers believe there were once as many as 300, with fire, tornado or time felling them before they were recorded. Today the Indiana Department of Natural Resources keeps track of the diminishing number still standing, counting fewer than 70 still in existence. Concerned that this piece of the state's history will soon be lost, Indiana Landmarks listed round barns on their Ten Most Endangered list.

The Van Nuys barn was added to the National Register of Historic Places, along with nineteen other round barns. The group is representative of the various construction types and styles found in the state. The Van Nuys barn was built from concrete blocks, a seldom-used material in barn construction.

Andrew Van Nuys came to Boone County from southern Indiana. He married Harvenia Frances Mount and moved to Lebanon in 1866. Harvenia's brother, James Mount, was governor of the state from 1896 to 1900. Andrew and Harvenia built an Italianate brick house on the property in 1882, and over time their farm grew to be 162 acres. Andrew built his round barn in 1913 at the age of seventy-six. The circular structure is 50 feet in diameter, 160 feet in circumference and 17 feet tall from the ground

The Andrew Van Nuys Barn is the only round barn remaining in the county and the only one made of concrete block remaining in the state. *Courtesy of the* Lebanon Reporter.

to the roof eaves. The barn measures 2,000 square feet and is supported by eight interior posts. The roof was originally slate but has been replaced with other material over the years. He died six years after his barn was built and was buried in Oak Hill Cemetery next to Harvenia, who died in 1891. The barn is now privately owned and unreachable to the general public.

The round barn was not only picturesque but also functional and efficient. Livestock, such as cattle, could be organized on the outer perimeter, with food in the center. The circular inner ring could be traversed by wagons, which wouldn't need to backtrack after passing each stall. Dairy farmers were fond of using round barns and placing milking stalls around the outer perimeter. The inner ring could serve as an indoor exercise track for horses during poor weather. The circular barn provided more space with the same amount of material as a rectangular one. Many circular barns were constructed with balloon framing. More than half of the Indiana barns were true circles, versus polygonal variations, such as the common twelve-sided and eight-sided structures.

Most of these barns were made from pliable wood to form the curved walls. On occasion, barns were constructed of glazed tile, poured concrete and, in one instance, brick. Three barns in the state were constructed with concrete blocks; the last to survive is located in Boone County. The Van Nuys barn is also known as the Quellhorse Barn or the Kincaid Barn, so named for its previous owners.

The popularity of the round barn began to wane after World War I. By 1929 construction of any kind halted. By the time the Great Depression was over, it was far more common for existing barns to be reused or new barns made with inexpensive materials. The round barn, with its unique siding and structural support, was no longer desirable.

Boone County had one other round barn on record. Indiana's first circular silo barn was built in Boone County in 1894 in Jefferson Township. Circular silos in the center of the round barn helped stabilize the structure and made it easier for the material in the silos to flow. This barn was destroyed in the 1990s.

Chapter 19

Scotland Bridge

In the midst of a wooded area surrounded by farmland in Clinton Township is a limestone bridge over Sugar Creek, the only masonry bridge in the county and one of the few remaining stone arch bridges in Central Indiana. A long gravel road leads to it from Boone County, turning into a newly paved road in Clinton County on the other side.

Scotland Bridge, built in 1901, was a primary transportation route across Sugar Creek. It provided access to the Scotland Church and cemetery across the waterway, both important to the Scotch-Irish immigrants who had settled in the area. The church was built in 1894, and for several years there was no simple and stable access across Sugar Creek for members of the community. In 1901 citizens petitioned the county commissioners to build the bridge, even offering to contribute funding to the project. It took fewer than five months at a cost of around $4,000 to complete. The county also considered bids for metal bridge options with a less expensive price tag, but the swampy site would have required solid foundations for every footing four feet below the creek bed. Public sentiment leaned toward the stone option.

When the bridge was completed, it had four round arches spanning twenty-seven feet each. In 1908, despite the solid stone foundation, three of the four arches had become compromised by Sugar Creek's current. The three arches were replaced with only two arches of the same size. The foundation was fortified with concrete and aprons.

Today, Scotland Bridge, one of 192 in the county, is infrequently used. It's surrounded by overgrown forest, with one of the arches nearly hidden

More than 120 years after being built, Scotland Bridge has fallen into disrepair. *Author's photo.*

beneath brush and sand. The sides of the bridge have crumbled, and the foundational repairs from 1908 have worn to the point that it is no longer structurally sound. The old bridge was originally built to support the weight of horses and carriages, and heavier vehicles and farm equipment have taken their toll. The county has investigated repairing it or rerouting traffic, but the bridge's future is bleak.

The gravel road that crosses the bridge traveling north out of Boone County has its own curious story and speculation. The road today is known as County Road North 200 East but its more romantic and notable name is the Lost Road.

Some believe the Lost Road to be so named because the road disappeared into the swamp before the bridge was built. An 1876 map shows the road continuing on to the other side, indicating that either a bridge or a ford was on the site at one point. Others believe it has something to do with lost souls along the route. The road originally began along the Strawtown Road and then headed north across Sugar Creek, stopping at the base of a tree. Anecdotally, the tree was said to be large enough that a person could sleep in its hollowed trunk to rest before returning—no longer lost—to civilization.

PART III.

MYTHS AND LEGENDS

CHAPTER 20

DIXON AND CAPADOCIA

Just off the road in Thorntown, on a private farm, two bushes flank a short cement pillar topped with a plaque that commemorates the location of a "Miami Indian Cemetery." It is said to mark the graves of two chiefs, Capadocia and Dixon, who perished in 1829.

According to *History of Boone County* by L.M. Crist, written in 1914, these two chiefs of the Eel River Band were at odds about the treaty signed in 1828 that would give the Thorntown Reserve to the government and require them to vacate the area. It is said that when Dixon signed the treaty, it angered Capadocia (or Chap-a-do-sia, as it is spelled in Crist's book). The two reportedly fought with hunting knives, plunging them into one another at the same time. The story was recounted that both died instantly, staring into one another's eyes with hatred. The tale further relays that they were buried in a shallow grave, per the Miami tradition, facing one another in a sitting position with their feet nearly touching. Their graves are said to contain the materials they would need for the hunting grounds in their next life: knives, tomahawks, rifles and their favorite hunting dogs and horses.

It's a tragic tale, but how much is true?

The names Dixon, Chap-a-do-sia and Capadocia do not appear in the 1828 treaty, which contains the names of seventeen other prominent Eel River leaders. Although the marker notes that their deaths happened in 1829, it's believed the Eel River band were forced to leave the area by the end of 1828. A man named Dixon, also known as Metakequah, was

A marker outside of Thorntown notes the graves of two chiefs. *Author's photo.*

associated with the Eel River band. It's unknown if he had a leadership role, but his death was reported in 1846.

A prominent Miami figure known as Captain Dixon had a brother known as Champadosia, or Šaapontohsia in the Miami language, a name which could have been confused for Capadocia. However, records from the Miami Nation show that Šaapontohsia and his descendants were still living in the Marion area in the 1850s. Although this Dixon was murdered by knife in 1839 in northern Indiana, it wasn't at the hand of his brother.

Perhaps the account of this Dixon's death was confused with the former Eel River resident. Or perhaps the tale was mingled with another story from Boone County, reported in the *Jamestown Press* in 1898. The article, based on a story in the *Thorntown Argus*, relayed a legend of two young Eel River men who died at one another's hands. The two were fighting over a young woman; the *Jamestown Press* stated that she "refused to show either the preference." The young men met near a cemetery and fought with arrows, then knives, "until each fell over dead." The graves were briefly unearthed in 1836 by the Kenworthy family, who at the time owned land slightly northwest of Thorntown. The graves were immediately covered, and the family took pains not to disturb this or other burial areas on their property.

Although the true story will likely never be known, three areas of Thorntown are recognized as being part of larger burial grounds, including the one memorialized with the monument for Dixon and Capadocia, an area which must have had some significant meaning. Those who moved to Thorntown shortly after the treaty was signed recounted that members of the Eel River band brought food to the site daily. They also said that, for many years, the location was a place of annual pilgrimage.

CHAPTER 21

A GORILLA IN THE MIDST

In the summer of 1949, there were reports throughout Thorntown about a gorilla that had been spotted in the woods near a popular fishing spot along Sugar Creek. For weeks, hunts were organized that yielded nothing, while the mysterious creature continued to be spotted in other locations in the area.

On July 17 the mystery was solved, when a reportedly "demented," unwashed woman with matted hair and a dark dress was found near the creek. When she was apprehended, she was said to have asked the town marshals, "Do you think I have scared them long enough?"

The possibility of a gorilla roaming Thorntown had gained national attention, and hundreds of volunteers combed the area, hoping to either catch it or catch a glimpse. Children were prevented from going outdoors, and family members were terrified to leave their homes. The woman's capture seemed to be the end of it. It wasn't until years later in the 1960s, during a presentation at a Kiwanis Club meeting, that Thorntown resident Asher Cones made a confession.

"The Thorntown Gorilla was an accident," he said.

Cones said that he, along with two other friends, George Coffman and Homer Birge, decided to scare local avid fisherman Gobby Jones. Jones spent all his free time fishing along the banks of Sugar Creek and often boasted about his success there. The men wanted to frighten him enough to drive him away from the spot for a while so others could enjoy it.

Birge and his wife built an animal costume from two old horsehair coats and a pair of overalls. They used wire and papier-mâché to create a head with glassy eyes. They intended it to look like a bear and knew the suit wouldn't pass a close inspection—but, as Cones stated, none of their victims stuck around for very long.

Once the costume was complete, the men set the trap. Coffman brought Jones to a prearranged spot, where the "gorilla" stood up and surprised him.

"It scared Gobby so bad that he climbed a bank that he normally could not have climbed no matter how hard he tried," reported Cones.

The prank was so successful that the men decided to try tricking others. They began popping up all over town, primarily focused on those who were skeptical. Birge and Coffman claimed they'd seen the gorilla, but Cones took the role of chiding those who believed the tall tale. Thus they hoped to keep the prank alive. All three men took turns in the gorilla suit, so that none could be accused of being the ape.

As the story grew over the next several weeks, groups of residents began to search for the gorilla. Cones, Birge and Coffman ensured that at least one of them was always in the hunting party to throw the group off the trail. In the meantime, another of the three would don the suit and appear in a completely different part of town.

Then things became more serious. Visitors from out of town gathered to assist with formal search parties. Planes circled overhead to widen the search area. With the mounting pressure of being caught, the men decided to quit. They put the suit in a box, nailed the box shut and hid it in an attic. No one knows where the suit resides today or if it even still exists.

Even after the men stopped, there were reports of gorilla sightings until the bedraggled woman was found in the same spot where the gorilla had been seen earlier in the summer. That's when the story finally died.

The three men kept their silence for a while once they realized they'd upset some of their neighbors. Some had even lost work because family members were too afraid to drive. But Cones contends that they made sure they only tried to frighten the people they knew.

As for the captured woman, she was only ever identified as being in her forties. Her name was withheld in all newspapers "to avoid embarrassing her family," according to authorities. They stated that she was to be sent to a mental institution.

This wasn't the only incidence of Boone County residents donning costumes to frighten their neighbors. In 1864 in the little town of Mechanicsburg, further east along Sugar Creek, friends Alderson

Garrett and Jasper Gipson were fishing near a small cemetery near Lost Road. They were enjoying time at home before they were due to join the Union Army.

The two noticed that the cemetery's normally thick green grass had been recently grazed. Consequently, some monuments had been overturned, and graves had been trampled. As night was approaching, the boys devised a plan to frighten the culprit if he returned.

They went to Alderson's home to ask his mother and sister to help outfit them in robes. The boys collected stilts they had recently built, and along with their costumes, they returned to the cemetery. They hid behind a mound of dirt, waiting for darkness. It wasn't too long before a man known as Newt Smith arrived with his horse and immediately allowed it to munch upon the grass. The boys wordlessly climbed atop the pile of dirt, covered themselves in robes and stood on the stilts. Spotting them, Newt let out a yell, grabbed his horse and fled to the general store, where he told the small crowd that generally gathered there that he had seen tall twin ghosts in the graveyard.

After a deal of discussion, the crowd decided to return to the cemetery the following night. Newt was so shaken and terrified that they seemed to believe there was some truth to his story. Hearing both the plan to return and the effect their prank had on Newt, the boys decided to appear once more. They heard the voices of the crowd coming and stood again atop the pile of dirt, against a pale moon. The group of visitors spotted them and fled in terror, just as Newt had.

The following day, the story spread beyond the town. A group planned to visit the cemetery once again that evening, this time armed with guns. The joke was no longer worth continuing. Alderson and Jasper feigned surprise whenever they heard the story but kept the truth quiet. It might have gone unknown if Alderson's niece hadn't recounted it later in life.

Chapter 22

Monkey Business

Years ago, when Michelle Howden chaperoned her daughter's third-grade walking tour of Zionsville, the guide commented on a town rumor.

"This just might be Zionsville legend, but we heard there was once a monkey on Main Street," said the guide.

Michelle raised her hand.

"This is my story," Michelle announced. "I'll take over here."

In 1964 the Howden children—Muff, Michal and Michelle—were being introduced to their potential new home on Willow Road, just north of Zionsville's Main Street. The children were on the back porch when Esther Shelburne, the home's current owner, brought a banana from the kitchen.

Esther placed it on the railing and told the children to watch. Within minutes a rhesus monkey emerged from a nearby tree and made his way to the fruit, snatching it and scrambling back up the bark. The children were astounded.

The most likely source of the monkey appears to be the former Pittman-Moore laboratory, just south of Zionsville. In 1954 Pittman-Moore was one of five facilities in the country producing the new polio vaccine. The kidney tissue from monkeys was used to support the growth of the vaccine. Although several types of monkeys were used, the rhesus macaque monkey was one of the most common.

It appears that a group of monkeys escaped from the facility in 1959. Pittman-Moore contended that every missing animal had been caught,

The escaped rhesus monkey was known to ride horseback. *Courtesy of the SullivanMunce Cultural Center.*

despite reports that at least one was still living on the Shelburne property. According to a Columbus, Indiana newspaper, the company stated, "It is not ours, we caught them all."

And so the Shelburne family, and then the Howden family, learned to live with a monkey, and its presence soon became routine.

"It was like seeing squirrels in the trees," said Muff.

The Howden children would often introduce the monkey to friends through the same banana trick, sometimes startling them. The family and community became accustomed to seeing the monkey, and Michael said it was fairly famous around town.

The monkey was occasionally seen riding on the back of their horse and trying to mother their kittens. The experience wasn't always pleasant. Michelle remembers the monkey once carrying a kitten to the top of the barn, expecting it to be able to climb on its own. The kitten instead fell to the ground to its death.

The monkey slept in their barn and spent most of its time there. Muff said that everyone knew they had a monkey in town, but it never seemed to leave their property. They heard reports of their dog visiting the local pharmacy, Jones Meat Market or the Friendly restaurant. Their horse was known to let himself out and wander Main Street. But no one ever complained about the monkey.

The monkey was finally captured around 1970 when it ventured a block away and crashed a children's birthday party, terrorizing the guests. The Indianapolis Zoo soon apprehended it and added it to their exhibit.

This wasn't the only incidence of a rogue monkey in town, which could have contributed to the many stories and rumors about monkeys riding atop pigs or climbing church steeples and ringing bells. In 1954 a single fugitive monkey was shot in Zionsville. It had climbed atop the Methodist Church and was "showing off," according to the *Indianapolis Star*. The church pastor reported that the directive was given in order to prevent the monkey from doing damage to the property overnight.

The following year, another monkey escaped from a shipment from India. This monkey lived for ten years on another farm, owned by the Plew family, northwest of Zionsville. The female was also reported to mother kittens and carry them into trees, sometimes accidentally causing them to fall to their deaths. It was eventually captured by the zoo but became a small media sensation because it validated a theory from Russian scientists. They had recently reported that tropical species can adapt to cold climates when required, something at least two of these monkeys had managed to prove.

Chapter 23

Haunted Bridges

Like virtually every community, there are places in Boone County rumored to be haunted. One in particular is the Holliday Drive Bridge, also known as the Holliday-O'Neal Bridge.

The bridge is located along Holliday Drive in the Holliday Farms subdivision. For decades, passersby would report strange happenings from the bridge, whether hearing screams of children or a car's engine failing suddenly while cruising it. Paranormal expert Nicole Kobrowski has authored more than a dozen books on unusual experiences in Indiana, including this bridge. Her extensive research has unearthed no deaths or tragedies associated with the bridge that might indicate unusual experiences.

While one rumor is that the bridge was the site of a Ku Klux Klan lynching, there were no reports of such an incident in that area, nor does the bridge appear to be tall enough to hang someone.

The bridge was originally built in 1892 and restored in 2008. It was damaged on December 2, 2017, when an attachment on a farm tractor caught a section of bridge, causing it to collapse. The driver's insurance refused to pay, so the county spent more than $1 million on repairs in 2019.

It's possible that this bridge has been confused in lore with the Screaming Bridge, a pony truss bridge over Eagle Creek near Willow Road. The rumors of hauntings date back many decades, beginning with a tale that a woman threw herself from the bridge, falling to her death. Other rumors say that she was pushed. Some say that gasoline was poured on the bridge and lighted, but the bridge never burned nor showed signs of being scorched.

Further north along Michigan Road, another ghost sighting is rumored with no substantive evidence. At the intersection of U.S. Route 421 and State Road 32, before the roundabout was constructed, drivers reported seeing several nuns walking in single file from one side of the road to the other.

Kobrowski notes that such tales handed down over decades and even centuries often have an element of truth, but the location or facts around the stories will frequently shift over time.

CHAPTER 24
THE COURTHOUSE TUNNEL

Beneath Lebanon's courthouse lies a long tunnel, connecting the building with the jail across the street. For many years it was rumored that the tunnel was once a pathway to move prisoners safely from the courthouse without exposure to the outdoors. It was imagined to be a small version of similar secret tunnels in Indianapolis or Washington, D.C. This imagined version seemed the only logical assumption.

While the existence of a tunnel is completely true, in fact it has never been used to transport prisoners. The tunnel was used to move heat from the boiler across the street in the jail into the large courthouse. Other wiring and infrastructure shared by the two buildings has been housed in the tunnel over the years. The tunnel was accessed by a hole in the ground and is roughly two feet by three feet on the courthouse side—just large enough to crawl through, but nothing more. Today the tunnel beneath the two buildings is inaccessible.

Young men starting their careers at the courthouse were tasked with clearing cobwebs from the pipes. One member of the county sheriff's department recalls the line of steam that would float from the street in the winter as the heated tunnel would melt the snow on top.

While there was no tunnel to transport prisoners, a cell was built between the third and fourth floors of the courthouse. It was a private space used to hold prisoners awaiting trial when the upper courtrooms were in use.

CHAPTER 25

HEADSTONES WITH NO GRAVES

One of Boone County's curiosities is an oft-speculated area in Zionsville. The route is frequently traveled, and occasionally questions will arise from new residents or those who are suddenly attentive: Why are there headstones at the corner of Mulberry Street and Turkey Foot Road?

Three small headstones occupy the corner, nestled in the dirt. Beyond the stones, behind a fence in front of a house, are three larger cemetery stones. John L. McCracken is the only legible name. But McCracken is buried in Indianapolis and, as far as anyone can tell, never lived in Zionsville.

So how did these stones appear in Boone County?

The home's original owner, Eugene Pock, was a heavy machine operator who, as part of his job, moved old headstones and gravestones, replacing them with new ones. As there was no use for the discarded stones, he was allowed to keep them. He decided they could be used as backfill for the steep slope by his house.

The house was eventually passed along to his granddaughter Jennifer Kelshaw and her husband, Gary. The stones were discovered in the early 2000s by pipeline workers who were working on the property. They were in the midst of digging but immediately stopped their work in a panic, according to Gary Kelshaw. Most of the stones remained along the hillside, but some were unearthed for a different use.

Three were prominently placed along the curve, in hopes that they would block cars from driving onto the property. Because the home is located along a tight curve, cars frequently misjudge the road. The stones were added after the corner fence had to be replaced due to an automobile crash. Gary Kelshaw said that the stones have stopped at least eight cars since their addition.

One motorcyclist decades ago wasn't so lucky, plowing into the side of the house when Pock lived there. Several boulders were put into the yard after that accident.

The couple doesn't have an estimate of how many other stones might be lying beneath the earth, but Pock's son told Kelshaw the yard is filled with them.

Many curious people have knocked on the Kelshaws' door to ask about the headstones, often nervous that there are bodies buried under the corner. Gary's response is always the same: "No, we don't have people buried here."

CHAPTER 26
GRAVES WITH NO HEADSTONES

Multiple Boone County locations once served as cemeteries but now have no headstones to mark the souls buried there. The most notable, and most likely the largest, is located in Lebanon. When the town was created in 1832, no official cemetery was established, so the town set aside land to be used for a public burial ground half a mile from the town center. Some of the graves were marked with headstones, but some were left unidentified. With no one operating the cemetery, no records were kept, and there was no one tasked with maintaining it.

Eventually it became common for people to come upon a body when they were digging a new grave for a loved one. Historian Ralph Stark estimated in *Boone County Magazine* that at least 1,200 burials over the four decades "would be a conservative estimate."

As more people moved to Lebanon, the city limits began to encroach on the cemetery, and it fell into disrepair. In 1872 the city council determined that the land was full of bodies and no one was allowed to be buried there in the future. At the same time Samuel Rodefer decided to establish Rodefer Cemetery as an official burial ground for the community.

With the establishment of a new cemetery, some residents began to dig up their deceased relatives to be moved to the new burial ground. The entire process was very informal and unregulated. Quite often after removing a body, an unfilled hole remained, which resulted in many injuries. Over the next few decades, the newspapers would occasionally report when certain individuals were moved from one cemetery to the other, but that was the extent of recording the activity.

A group of women known as the Belles of 60 took it upon themselves to take care of the property in 1906. This group of women, so named because were young together in the 1860s, began to raise funds to maintain it. It was through their efforts that it was given the name Cedar Hill Cemetery in 1907. A year later they petitioned the city and were able to install a retaining wall around the land, which still exists today.

When the Belles ran out of money and their members began to pass away, it became a desolate area once again, called by some "a blight on the town." By the 1950s the town decided something had to be done. The Junior Chamber of Commerce, also known as the Jaycees, proposed turning the area into a park. Through a state law, they were able to legally have the headstones removed to a separate area, although the bodies remained. This law stated that an abandoned cemetery could be redesigned if no burials had taken place for a certain number of years. An aged and established resident of Lebanon confirmed the last burial he recollected, and the state allowed his testimony.

The Daughters of the American Revolution tracked all of the headstones as they were removed from the property starting in 1954, identifying names and dates whenever possible. Most headstones were worn and damaged. Those that were most legible were lined around the perimeter of the cemetery to serve as a barrier and honor the departed souls.

Over a very short period, those stones began to disappear, until suddenly they were all gone. Some may have been used as backfill. On occasion they have been found in areas of town like Sugar Creek, Prairie Creek and the Conservation Club.

Today it's unknown how many of the bodies were removed, but it's assumed that quite a few still remain. A marker stands on the property, noting that "over 500 citizens of early Lebanon including 32 war veterans sleep here. Remember us for we, too, once lived and served this community." The only other marker on the land holds the date 1776. It was installed in 1912 as part of an initiative to identify the graves of the county's Revolutionary War soldiers, and it marks the grave of James Hill, who settled in Lebanon after the war. It was the only new marker for decades and is the last such monument the county erected in this initiative. The cemetery is now renamed James Hill Memorial Park.

Jamestown has its own cemetery with no headstones, but local reports confirm that headstones once existed. Johns Cemetery has eight graves, but no one knows exactly where they are, and there's no official record of who was buried there. The cemetery is located southwest of First Street and

Cedar Hill Cemetery held the graves of Lebanon's earliest residents. *Author's photo.*

Four Winds Drive. A summary of Jamestown history written by Andrew K. Houk Sr. for the town's sesquicentennial lists five individuals who died in the 1850s; theirs are believed to be the names of the departed in that general location.

CHAPTER 27

DEAD MAN'S BRIDGE

Between Jamestown and Advance in the southwest corner of the county is a bridge known locally as Dead Man's Bridge. It crosses Raccoon Creek, which flows through pastures of cows and fields of corn and hay. It earned the moniker after a grisly discovery that led police to solve one of central Indiana's more horrific murders.

Alva Mitchell operated a farm in the area before nearby Interstate 74 was built. There were a number of dairy cows on the property, along with fields of crops. On the morning of April 11, 1946, it was time for milking, but a number of the cows were missing. Mitchell wandered the property, searching with no luck. He then decided to follow the creek bank and came upon some hoofprints. Tracing the hoofprints, he found the cows near a bridge and noticed something burning.

At the same time, former army infantryman Howard Troth was plowing a nearby field when he noticed a black sedan stop on a nearby bridge. Moments later, he saw something burning and thought the bridge was in flames. He reached the area about the same time as Mitchell, and they discovered that an old army blanket had been set on fire under the bridge. Troth kicked the blanket to extinguish the flames, and a human foot fell out, followed by two slender hands.

"He freaked out," recounted Mitchell's nephew, Rick Mitchell.

Troth and Mitchell called the police and went back to their work, unaware that their discovery would solve the murder of Leland Paul Miller. Miller's body had been hacked, with the separated head and torso discovered in a fire in Ladoga in Montgomery County. That fire had been set at an abandoned farm more than ten miles to the west earlier that day. The hands and feet had been removed in an attempt to prevent anyone from easily identifying the body.

Mitchell and Troth believed the murderers would have gotten away with the crime if they hadn't set the fire under the bridge. "If they had built the fire in the bushes a little distance from the bridge we'd probably never have paid any attention to them," Mitchell told the *Indianapolis News*.

The hands and foot being wrapped in a blanket protected them long enough to prevent them from becoming charred and the fingerprints untraceable. Miller's left foot was disabled, which would have also made identification of the body easier.

Troth also identified the black sedan, leading police on a hunt for Howard Pollard and Harold Tanner, two men who had been associated with Miller. The men were arrested and tried in a case that became known as the "hands-and-foot slaying."

The old metal bridge was removed and replaced in 1999, but it still retains its grim moniker among locals.

As for the trial, Pollard was tried and convicted in the murder, which he claimed was self-defense after Miller attempted to stab him with a knife. In a strange twist a year earlier, Miller had been arrested for shooting Pollard through the neck after both men attempted to assault a female, forcing her into their car. Pollard had been arrested eighteen previous times, but observers believe those cases were dismissed because of the Pollard family's political influence.

Chapter 28

Lebanon Cedars?

Boone County is home to three high schools represented by three very different mascots.

The most recent of the three schools, Western Boone Junior-Senior High School, was established in 1974 to consolidate students from Dover, Pinnell, Thorntown, Washington and Granville Wells Schools. The five schools are represented by the five points of their mascot, the star Orion.

Zionsville Community High School's mascot is named the Eagle, likely named for Eagle Creek and Eagle Township, where an abundance of eagles once lived. The school has existed since 1885—when it was known as the Academy, where the town's library is now situated—but it was forty years before the school associated itself with a mascot. The "Zionsville Eagles" nickname was first found in print on November 9, 1925, in *Walnut Chips*, as the heading for the school's upcoming basketball schedule.

While eagles and stars are often seen in central Indiana, tigers are not quite as common. How was Lebanon's mascot chosen?

Lebanon High School was established in 1876. Fifty years later, with interest in team mascots growing across the country, they took steps to establish one of their own. In November 1926, the students voted from a list of five possible mascots, all suggested by members of the student body. Their choices were Cedars, Oreoles, Mohawks, Greyhounds and Tigers. In all, 145 students voted in a very close race. The least popular option,

Oreoles, received only eleven votes. Greyhounds followed with twenty-five votes. It came down to the final three choices, with Cedars and Mohawks receiving thirty-six votes each. Ultimately Tigers, with thirty-seven votes, won the contest. Had any of those voting for Tigers selected differently, it's likely the fans would be cheering alongside a very different mascot today.

CHAPTER 29

WILL THE REAL CENTER OF INDIANA PLEASE STAND UP?

For a short time, Boone County was noted as being both the geographic and population center of the state, the latter being the point where there are an equal number of people living in every direction.

In 1980 the state's population center was calculated and noted to be near the northeast corner of Boone County, between Michigan Road and the Hamilton County line. The distinction was short lived. Within a decade the population growth shifted south and then east into Hamilton County, a result of factories and manufacturing facilities closing in the northern part of the state.

The recognition and distinction as the geographic center began as early as 1966, when a mile marker was erected in Eagle Township by the Indiana Sesquicentennial Commission. It pinpointed the geographic center of the state on Michigan Road, just a mile and a half north of State Road 334 in Zionsville. The marker read: "Geographic Center of Indiana: This spot was once the center of the town of Clarkston (or Hamilton), Eagle Township, Boone County, which was abandoned about 1880."

The marker was damaged in the 1990s and removed by the Indiana Historical Bureau in 1995. The sign was determined to be unrepairable and was not replaced. Staff at the IHB confirmed that challenges surrounding the determination of a geographic center have made the claim impossible to substantiate and likely contributed to why it was never replaced.

Boone County's distinction has since been challenged by other sources. Wikipedia currently lists a location in Hendricks County as the center. In

1982 a Cincinnati mapmaker designated a corner in Greenwood to be the center. Another website puts the center of the state less than three miles to the south of the Boone County border.

The United States Geological Society, once the determining body for such a distinction, states:

> *There is no generally accepted definition of geographic center, and no completely satisfactory method for determining it. Because of this, there may be as many geographic centers of a State or country as there are definitions of the term…because many factors, such as the curvature of the earth, large bodies of water, and irregular surfaces, affect the determination of centers of gravity, the following positions should be considered as approximations only.*

The USGS includes a listing of their calculated locations of the center of each state. For Indiana, Boone County's spot fourteen miles northwest of Indianapolis proudly holds that honor.

PART IV.

INFLUENCERS

CHAPTER 30
THE LEGACY OF ANSON MILLS

Thorntown's public water system was built thanks to a former resident's interest in weaving.

Anson Mills was born August 31, 1834, in Thorntown. His family were farmers and weavers, and he learned both skills growing up in the community. In 1852 he left Indiana to attend Charlottesville Academy in Virginia, then received an appointment to West Point a few years later.

After leaving the military academy he was hired to survey a town in Texas that was planned to be called Franklin. He platted the town and was asked to rename it, which he did based on its location as the north and south pass of the Rio Grande through the Rocky Mountains. He thus earned the nickname "Father of El Paso." In 1961, he left Texas to fight in the Civil War, then led multiple campaigns with the U.S. Army and eventually rose to the rank of brigadier general.

In the early 1880s he combined his military experience and his looming skills to create what he called "my greatest material achievement." He had become frustrated with the quality of the cartridge belts required by the U.S. military. The leather would negatively impact copper in cartridges, and the belt would stretch when wet, not ideal for soldiers in outdoor conditions. He developed a woven version that addressed these issues. In 1881 he patented the design, which was used by the United States Army and Navy and the Canadian military. The Mills Woven Cartridge Belt Company prospered, and he was able to sell it in 1905, allowing him to retire comfortably.

Mills Fountain was unveiled October 7, 1909. *Courtesy of the Thorntown Heritage Museum.*

And so, in 1908, when Mills returned to Thorntown with his wife, Nannie, he was prepared to make a lasting donation to the community. A local minister was eager to meet with Mills, hoping that he would donate a library, which the town badly needed. At the time Thorntown was facing a crisis. The town had been built over impervious clay, which extended twenty feet below the surface. This poor drainage contributed to contaminated wells and a resulting outbreak of typhoid.

Coincidentally, Nannie Mills had recently recovered from typhoid, and Anson believed his money could be more useful in building a pure water system than building a library. He proposed the idea to the town on one condition: that they would maintain a large fountain erected in memory of his parents. The town enthusiastically agreed.

Mills designed an additional drinking fountain to be positioned at the opposite end of the street from the large fountain. It was designed with a tall tier for horses and small bowl below for dogs. He also contributed at least two fountains for humans.

When the fountains were complete, the town held an unveiling celebration on October 7, 1909. Mills attended along with his family, distant relatives and an estimated ten thousand people. Considering the town's population was around two thousand, it's believed that the other visitors were wealthy friends of Mills traveling by train from across the country to witness the event.

The fountains were a popular attraction for many years but fell into disrepair, proving to be too expensive to maintain. The horse drinking fountain was damaged in 1914, so the town contacted the foundry to have it repaired. Because it had been a special order, the repair cost was too great for the small community to afford. In 1939 the horse fountain was filled with dirt and flowers to maintain some attractiveness.

Through the years both fountains required repairs to the concrete and paint to prevent rust. In early 1942 it was discovered that bolts attaching the figures on the Memorial Fountain to the base had completely rusted. Wires were used to hold them temporarily in place, but one evening the wires were cut and the next morning the statues were found in pieces in the basin. Thorntown resident Roy Fairfield offered to remove the statues and purchase the metal scrap. The town agreed to let him remove the drinking

The horse fountain had a smaller bowl below for dogs. *Courtesy of the Thorntown Heritage Museum.*

fountain but attempted to maintain the Memorial Fountain by converting the base into a planter.

In October 1942 the state highway commission approached the town to create a highway along Main Street. That would require completely removing the statues, which the town didn't want to do without approval from General Mills's family. Mills had only one surviving daughter, Constance Mills Overton. It took nearly two years to find her and come to a solution for the road. Constance agreed that the fountains should be removed, saying it was something her father would have supported. "He always rejoiced in anything contributing to the greater good, and tried to better each place he lived in," she wrote in a letter to the director of traffic in Indianapolis.

The head is all that remains from the original Mills Fountain. *Author's photo.*

The fountain's metal was melted for the war effort, and the fountain's plaques were placed in Town Hall. The statue's head is the only other piece that was preserved and can be seen today in Thorntown's Heritage Museum.

In 2002, as part of a library expansion, funds were raised to build a reproduction of Mills's fountain. The original fountain plans were discovered, and Robinson Iron in Alabama created a smaller replica made of cast aluminum. At twelve feet tall, it's only a fraction of the original thirty-two-foot height. The reproduction fountain was installed in 2007 and was filled with water on August 31, coincidentally Mills's birthdate.

Chapter 31

Riley's Boone County White Corn

J ames Riley didn't begin as a crop farmer, but he's remembered for creating one of the most popular and high-yielding corn varieties still in use today. His white corn variety is credited with adding thousands of dollars to the value of corn crops.

Riley grew up on a southern Indiana farm and moved to Thorntown in 1853. He was well known for breeding livestock, but in particular, he was known for breeding Chester white swine and Cotswold sheep. Around 1870 he noticed that breeders of Berkshire swine weren't particularly successful in reproducing their numbers, so he decided to breed them with the Poland China variety. For a decade he patiently tinkered with breeding, and within ten years his resulting breed was so improved that he produced more prize-winning hogs than any other farm at the time, some weighing up to nine hundred pounds. He was equally successful in breeding chickens, such as the Partridge Cochin and Plymouth Rock, winning additional accolades at several state fairs.

As he was perfecting his approach to adapting swine, he decided to channel what he'd learned into his relatively small field of seed corn on 108 acres. At the time very little had been done to improve on varieties of corn. In 1874 Riley crossed the county's most popular variety of white corn, known as White Mastodon, with another white corn variety. He ensured dead and diseased ears were quickly culled to allow the strongest plants to thrive. Over the next decade he continued this careful cultivation, strengthening the variety and crossing it with other breeds that matured earlier. The resulting

James Riley in his seed corn catalog. *Courtesy of the SullivanMunce Cultural Center.*

white corn was relatively massive in size at nearly a foot long, sturdier and produced a higher yield. At the height of their business the Riley family boasted that it could yield up to 125 bushels per acre, which was the highest yielding corn on record in its day. Today's crops yield an average of 115. Riley named the corn Boone County White Corn. It's used for cornmeal, feeding livestock and eating.

James and his son Marley began their own seed business, James Riley & Son. They described the Boone County White Corn in their seed pamphlets: "It is a pure white corn, all white cobs, grain deep, thick and meaty, well filled over butt and tip, stalk of medium height, thick and strong, seldom ever blows down and is remarkably yieldly."

Soon after working with white corn, James began experimenting with a yellow variety, creating a hybrid of golden yellow and Sibley's Pride of the North. This combination of a late yielding corn with an early yielding one resulted in a smaller ear of corn, but one with a very high yield. He called it Riley's Favorite Pedigreed Corn, primarily used to feed livestock.

In 1885 he brought both of his new varieties to a Chicago agricultural exposition, with both winning top honors in their respective yellow and white categories. In 1893 he received a gold medal for his yellow and white hybrids at the World's Fair in Chicago and a few years later received the same honor at the St. Louis Exposition.

Riley wasn't the only family member to find success at the World's Fair. His second wife, Mary Baldwin Riley, was an expert maker of dairy butter and received gold medals in Chicago that same year.

Chapter 32

Ace

Boone County honors many of its war heroes as far back as the Revolutionary War. One hero's grave is unknown, his beginnings unsure, but his contribution still remembered.

Donald Spees was a teenager when he acquired his dog Ace, reported by the *Zionsville Times* as "a combination of police, collie, and shepherd." Donald was too young to enlist when the United States joined World War II. Instead, Donald's father applied for Ace to join the army.

The program, called Dogs for Defense, began in 1942 to utilize dogs in the war effort and have them take specific tasks to replace human counterparts. Dogs served as sentries and scouts, guided first aid units to wounded soldiers and carried ammunition.

Dogs for Defense made many pleas in local newspapers and attended dog shows, hoping that owners would be willing to send their pets. Advertising encouraged youth to participate in dog donation as a sacrifice they could make to do their part for the war. Although ads also promoted that "one dog is equal to two men," by some estimates from those on the front lines, one dog could do the job of six men. At first any breed was accepted, provided they met the minimum requirements of being between one and five years old, weighing fifty pounds and standing twenty inches high at the shoulder. The program later narrowed their requirements to four breeds: German shepherds, Doberman pinschers, giant schnauzers or terriers and collies. These breeds had traits that made them more suitable for guarding and scouting, plus they had other useful attributes such as a keen sense

Many pets enlisted in Dogs for Defense were trained at Fort Royal, Virginia. *From the National Archives.*

of smell and hearing. Eventually only males were accepted because they tended to be more aggressive.

Dog owners near Indianapolis would bring their pets to the city's freight yard, where they would be crated and set on a train to boot camp either in Fort Royal, Virginia, or Fort Robinson, Nebraska. Dogs received an identifying tattoo on their leg, along with dog tags.

In April 1943, Ace got his chance. When he enlisted, Indiana had already sent 522 dogs to serve their country, and the state was leading the country in dog volunteers. Ace was among those sent to Virginia, where he spent nine weeks in boot camp. While it's unknown exactly where he was stationed, the Spees family believes Ace was in the Philippines and served as a sentry along enemy lines. These dogs would accompany guards walking the perimeter of military facilities and growl softly when they heard something.

Ace spent more than a year away from Zionsville and appears to be the only veteran dog in Boone County. The Spees family would joke that, as Ace had a history of fighting with other dogs, he was being sent to continue fighting for the United States. Despite his toughness with other animals, the

Zionsville newspaper stated that he was "a smart, nice appearing canine with a good disposition around children."

In early August 1944, Ace returned to the family. Donald reported that when they opened the cage in downtown Indianapolis, where Ace was delivered, it was like he had never been gone. It wasn't long after that when Donald himself was sent to fight in the Navy.

By the end of the war more than eighteen thousand dogs had served their country, of which about half were donated by families. Not all dogs returned home. An estimated two thousand of these dogs were killed in service, including some Indiana canines who were reported to have contracted tropical illnesses or incurable infections.

The Spees family remembers Ace as being an extremely smart dog, carrying a dime in his mouth to the local butcher in exchange for a bone and once saving a child who was drowning. While it's possible that Ace saved someone's life, it's also possible that the story was confused with a similar account of Donald saving the life of Edward Neese in December 1941. Donald had been watching a group of boys skate on the frozen water that filled a pit near town. The ice broke, and while other boys were able to scamper to safety, Edward fell in and couldn't swim. He grasped the broken edge of the ice as Donald inched his way across on his stomach and then dragged him to safety. The Boy Scouts commended Donald at a meeting in February, after Edward and other youngsters in the community recounted the tale. Donald was nonchalant about the heroic act. According to the *Zionsville Times*, "Spees laughed it off as 'nothing more than any boy scout would do.'"

Chapter 33
Thorntown Cyrus

One of Thorntown's oddest residents might be Thorntown Cyrus. He, and by association the town, were known throughout Indiana. Cyrus Marsh was born in New York in the early 1830s as the youngest of five children. When his mother became widowed, she moved her family to Indiana and eventually settled in Thorntown in the 1840s, living on Front Street. When Cyrus was young, he was stricken by a brain fever. His mother claimed that the doctor's placing cold ice on his warm head caused the damage, but more likely the illness damaged his brain and caused a form of dementia.

One by one his siblings left the home, until it was just Cyrus and his mother. His mother died in 1864, which furthered Cyrus's mental suffering. He began to drift to local fairs in communities farther and farther away from home, returning in the winter months to live in an old caboose back in Thorntown. In the 1880s he evidently burned the caboose after building a fire in the stove.

His time in these local fairs fascinated Cyrus. He soon grew eager to create an act of his own. He learned to play the accordion and trained a dog to perform. Other times he would don a dress and carry a parasol, parading as a woman. For more than twenty years, when the weather grew warm, Cyrus would migrate to other cities, such as Lafayette, Fort Wayne, Wabash, Tipton and Frankfort, pushing a large cart covered with draperies. The cart held pans, bedding and everything he needed to make it his roving home. It also housed a doll, approximately four feet tall, which followed him on his

Cyrus Marsh with his stereoscope. *Courtesy of the Tippecanoe Historical Society.*

travels. Some newspapers reported that dementia caused Cyrus to believe he was married and the doll was his wife. Others thought it represented his dead mother. Various reports say that the doll was made of wax, while others say it was made of rags. He called the doll Little Nell.

Everyone agreed that Cyrus was very protective of the doll. He was a relatively calm, quiet man unless people tried to disrupt his doll. The communities that Cyrus frequented seemed to be equally protective of him. The town of Lafayette passed an ordinance in which it became a misdemeanor to harass Cyrus.

Cyrus traveled from town to town with the intent of performing. He set his wagon near each community and would play the accordion—albeit poorly, speak of political and spiritual subjects, tell jokes or recite poems to entertain crowds. His small black dog, named Trippy, would perform while Cyrus played.

Cyrus was a bit of an inventor. He built an expertly crafted miniature guillotine based on a description he had heard. He created a stereoscope "peep show" of popular news events or a flood with rushing water. He watched carefully as a railroad was constructed and built his own life-sized rail car to use on the tracks.

In early March 1881, Cyrus caused quite a stir when he was found in his wagon near Frankfort, approximately fifteen miles from home, and believed to be dead. The newspapers reported his death, then corrected the reports the following week when he arrived in Thorntown unharmed. Rumors of his demise resurfaced in 1887 and 1888, when he hadn't been seen in Indiana and eastern Illinois towns during the summer months. One paper reported that he drowned when he and his wagon fell off a bridge. The paper speculated that he shied at a piece of paper while pretending to be a horse pulling his wagon, something he was known to do, and the cart tipped over the bridge, pulling Cyrus beneath the water.

In truth, Cyrus was admitted to the Boone County Infirmary around 1886 with a bout of tuberculosis. Community newspapers reported that he was an "inmate" of the facility and should be released to bring his act to the numerous towns who eagerly awaited his return during the warm months of the year. Instead, he remained in the infirmary until his death on May 21, 1889. Before he died, he reported that his age was fifty-eight. He was appropriately buried next to his mother in Thorntown.

Despite his illness, Cyrus had moments of lucidity. A tale was recounted in the *Lafayette Journal and Courier* in 1984. During a visit to Lafayette, one man kindly offered to pay for Cyrus's meal, placing a quarter on the counter.

The owner of the establishment tried to return it, insisting that he never charged Cyrus for food. The men continued to argue until Cyrus reached over and took the quarter, placing it in his own pocket. He reportedly said, "Far be it from me to see my best friends quarrel over such a matter."

CHAPTER 34

CAMPBELL, SMITH AND RITCHIE

Many are familiar with Hoosier cabinets, the stand-alone cabinet that could be custom-made for any kitchen. "Hoosier cabinet" has become a generic term for these über-customizable baking cabinets manufactured by roughly three dozen companies, most located in Indiana. One of the most popular versions was the Boone cabinet, made in Lebanon.

Campbell-Smith-Ritchie Company manufactured Boone cabinets for at least three decades. The business first began as a mill and lumberyard established in 1867. George Campbell purchased the mill along with partner Frank Coombs around 1892. Soon Coombs sold his share to James P. Smith, who had previously owned a lumberyard in northwest Indiana. In 1900 Morris Ritchie sold his Lebanon grocery business and joined Campbell and Smith in the endeavor. While their primary business was milling and lumber, they also made door and window frames and decorative trim.

The men had recently begun to dabble in creating kitchen cabinets when a fire in 1905 completely destroyed the mill and all their materials. They rebuilt on West South Street, adjacent to the Big Four Railroad. By 1907 they had incorporated the business and added furniture and cabinets to their collection. Within a few years, they decided to discontinue their lumber manufacturing and center all resources completely on the rapidly growing cabinet industry. In the 1920s, Boone cabinets could be purchased for as

Above: Campbell-Smith-Ritchie manufactured Boone cabinets in Lebanon for several decades, employing 150 people at its peak. *From the collection of Harley Sheets.*

Opposite: The company advertised that their Boone Cabinets were designed by 369 women. *From the* Scranton Times, *1927.*

little as twenty-five dollars or up to more than one hundred dollars for a version with two electrical outlets, a clock and an ironing board.

Boone cabinets were similar to other Hoosier cabinets, with dozens of customizable features. These included a retractable metal top, a coffee mill, a knife sharpener, spice tins, a recipe holder, a flour mill and a pegboard. Cabinets could be ordered with glass or covered windows and would store utensils, dishes and kitchen staples.

What made the Boone cabinets stand out began with a simple marketing idea. An advertising campaign invited women to send letters suggesting needed improvements to kitchen cabinets. The Campbell-Smith-Ritchie Company placed an ad in the *Ladies' Home Journal*, hoping to generate ideas for their new cabinets. The company received suggestions from 369 women across the country. They took many of these ideas and incorporated them into the designs of their newest line of cabinets. They capitalized on the responses for their next campaign, promoting that the cabinets were designed by these 369 women. The idea that the cabinets were designed by women for women was turned into an inventive and successful campaign.

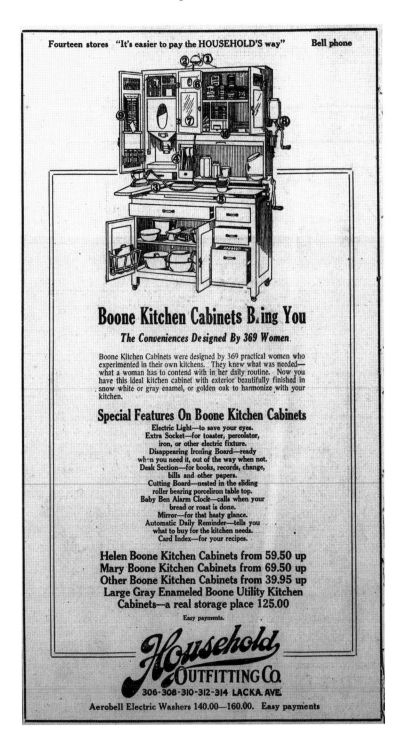

A few innovations made the Boone cabinets cutting edge for their time. Many of these features came standard with the top sellers, such as a built-in alarm clock, built-in desk, disappearing ironing board and electric light at the top. Others were extra, like a double electric socket and an Arcade Crystal coffee mill. The cabinets played upon women's vanity as well, with a hidden mirror tucked into the cabinet for a quick touchup "when the doorbell rings."

Different styles could fit different home configurations. One version with a utility closet at the end could be built into a wall. Another was only thirty-five inches high so that it could be placed below a kitchen window. Cabinets even came with a stool that could be tucked back into the cabinet quickly without taking up additional space. The cabinets also came in a variety of finishes: white enamel with green decoration, golden oak, gray oak or gray enamel with multiple colors of decorative designs at the top. Campbell-Smith-Ritchie Company then named these cabinets for women: Mary, Helen and Dorothy were some of the best-selling models.

Advertisements ran across the country in local newspapers and were most prevalent in the late 1920s. Many also boasted that the company was the oldest manufacturer of kitchen cabinets in the world. While not substantiated, the claim was very possibly true. The Hoosier Manufacturing Company in New Castle, Indiana, was on the heels of Campbell-Smith-Ritchie in creating storage options for kitchens. While the Hoosier Manufacturing Company was the first to create the Hoosier-style cabinet, both companies began manufacturing their separate built-in cabinets around the same time.

At its peak about 150 people worked for Campbell-Smith-Ritchie Company. Employees could receive a custom cabinet for free. Like most other kitchen cabinet manufacturers, the company's sales began to decline during the Great Depression. The company closed many manufacturing lines and focused on simply building built-in cabinets and oak breakfast tables and chairs.

Campbell and Ritchie were longtime Lebanon residents, but Smith never lived in Boone County. Campbell and Smith died in the 1910s. Ritchie worked for the company until it was sold to Eugene Burford Rhodes, an investor of another cabinetmaking company, in 1940. The business was bankrupt within a year.

Campbell-Smith-Ritchie Company was located just a few blocks from the center of Lebanon. Three Boone cabinets are on display at the Strange Cragun House, not far from where they were manufactured in the 1920s. Two were in the home when it was donated to the Boone County Historical

Society. Another found its way to Lebanon via an antique dealer hoping to find a home for the Boone cabinet she'd purchased but didn't know how to refurbish. She discovered the cabinet's manufacturer, which led her to the county historical society, and she generously donated the item back to the community where it was first built.

CHAPTER 35

HAROLD AND MELVIN HILLER

Melvin Hiller had journalism in his blood. His father, Harold Hiller, ran the *Jamestown Press* starting in 1917, when he purchased the paper after working there as a young man. Melvin grew up in the newsroom, sweeping the floors and learning how to set the press. In 1948 Melvin had recently returned from a tour of duty with the Fifth Air Force in the Occupational Forces in Japan when his father suffered a stroke. While it didn't take his life, it left the Hiller patriarch incapacited and unable to continue his newspaper work. Melvin Hiller didn't plan to stay in Jamestown and take over the family business, but he chose to follow in his father's footsteps. "I was 20 years of age when this job suddenly fell on me," Melvin Hiller once told his readers.

He knew some of the basics but relied upon assistance from his family, like his mother, Elsie, who helped with proofreading. His eventual wife, Joanne, learned to operate the Linotype machines that were used to print the newspaper on site. The Linotype was invented by Ottmar Mergenthaler, a German immigrant, in 1884 and was first used for publications by the *New York Tribune*. The invention revolutionized printing. The operator entered text onto a keyboard while the machine assembled the letterforms on the line. The assembly, called a slug, was cast for printing.

Even with the advancement of computers, Melvin continued to use any of three Linotype machines in the office, one of which dated to the early days of his father owning the newspaper. He always said he was raised on Linotype and therefore had no desire ever to change. Linotype was also

The Linotype machines used by the Hiller family are on display at the Jackson Township Historical Society. *Author's photo.*

called "hot type" because the machine forms typeset columns one line at a time from molten lead. By printing with the Linotype machines, he could publish the paper on site in Jamestown rather than sending it elsewhere. That meant he could cover news up until the last possible second before printing, rather than information that could be several days late.

In Hiller's role of editor, he was also publisher, reporter, photographer and printer. A one-man show running a weekly newspaper has its drawbacks. In 1968 Melvin was hospitalized with a kidney stone attack, and his wife and mother were by his side. Bob Pearcy, editor of the nearby *Danville Gazette*, and Harmon Hathaway, a former publisher of the *Coatesville Herald*, finished the work for their colleague. These small editors had a history of providing assistance for one another. When a tornado destroyed the plant of the *Coatesville Herald*, editors from the *Jamestown Press*, *Crawfordsville Journal* and *Zionsville Times* chipped in to ensure the publication was completed. Because of this sort of help from other editors, the *Jamestown Press* never missed an issue for the seventy-six years the Hiller family owned it. Melvin Hiller admitted that one issue was late during the blizzard of 1978, but even his father's stroke didn't prevent Melvin from ensuring the paper was released in 1948.

Melvin Hiller's last edition ran in January 1993, literally closing the doors on the oldest continually operating business in Jamestown. Even after closing the newspaper, Hiller still maintained the office and managed small printing jobs until 2001, when he sold the building and its contents to the Jackson Township Historical Society to create the state's first museum dedicated to the advancement of the newspaper.

The Linotype machines are still located in Hiller's former office along with printing tools and old editions of the *Jamestown Press*.

CHAPTER 36

WILLIAM DEVOL

As one of Lebanon's most prominent citizens, William DeVol climbed the ranks of the financial industry, moving from cashier to bank president of the First National Bank in a mere eight years. He was a stalwart in banking, but it seems he had a virtually untapped passion for architecture and design.

The DeVol family moved from Ohio to Lebanon with their four children in 1867, very soon after infant William was born. A few years later another son was added to the DeVol brood with the birth of Charles. As the two youngest in the family, brothers William and Charles had a close bond. When DeVol built a massive house in 1894 just a few blocks from Lebanon's courthouse, Charles built a home on the property next door. While William's house still stands today, unfortunately Charles's was destroyed by fire in 1914. William DeVol's home, known as Ingleside, has an impressive design with four fireplaces and pocket windows that slide into the walls.

William DeVol was popular in the community even as a youth, believed to be the first person in the county to own a bicycle. One summer afternoon in 1890, the young man pedaled back and forth across the graveled Main Street before a crowd of spectators, sparking a bicycle craze in town.

The community of Bayview, Michigan, credits William DeVol for helping them survive the Depression. In 1910 William and his wife, Josephine, were summering at the Nash Lodge outside of Petoskey when they learned that the lodge's owners were planning to retire and sell the hotel. Within hours he negotiated to buy the property and shortly purchased several adjoining parcels.

Their original plan was to modernize the dining room, but they soon discovered they needed to start fresh. They built a new forty-room hotel from the ground up and named it Terrace Inn. It was known as the area's "newest and most modern hotel," opening in 1911 with high-end features like running water, electric lights and rooms with private baths. The hotel was often used to house those on adult education Chautauqua tours, also a popular circuit in Boone County.

William DeVol. *Courtesy of Missy Krulik.*

The inn is still open today and is one of only two remaining hotels in the resort community. On the inn's property is a cottage that was the residence of the DeVol family when they stayed in Michigan. They christened the cottage "Nonabel," which is "Lebanon" spelled backwards.

As the DeVol family became more invested in the Michigan community, William decided to become a member of the Bay View Association in 1918. The association had accumulated a large amount of debt, and the community was in need of updated utilities. DeVol applied his financial expertise to help eliminate debt and manage the community's budget through the Depression, serving as treasurer until 1941. Without his involvement, the community could have gone bankrupt and the more than four hundred historic properties, many from the Victorian era, likely wouldn't exist today.

DeVol died suddenly from a heart attack while watching storm windows being installed on the exterior of his Lebanon home. After DeVol passed away, his home was converted into six rental apartments, run by one of his three daughters. It remained a rental until it was purchased by the Krulik family and converted into a single-family home. While exploring the home's basement, the Kruliks discovered a drafting table tucked into a corner. Inside was a time capsule, assumed to be untouched, as the piece of furniture was pushed aside when DeVol died. Among the treasures were a floor plan of the county courthouse, drafting tools, blueprints of his house, sketches of many Indianapolis homes and cottage home books.

DeVol's architectural interests reached far into the community. William served on the committee to build the county's new courthouse at the turn of the century and was on the board when Oak Hill Cemetery was formed.

William and Charles built several properties in Lebanon, including a building in the courthouse square that still stands.

DeVol's impact in both Indiana and Michigan lives on, as does his influence in many organizations. He was a popular citizen in Lebanon, well regarded in the community   except by a meat market owner on the east side. One evening in 1905, he was attacked by butcher Frank Shirley in an alley near the DeVol home. DeVol had just checked his sister's house across the street when Shirley attempted to asphyxiate the bank president. DeVol managed to escape, coming into the house brutally beaten. Shirley admitted to the crime but stated it was for a good reason, which he would share when the time was right. Throughout the trial, Shirley contended that DeVol knew what he did to deserve the assault, while the plaintiff claimed to know nothing of the matter. Shirley never shared his side of the story, and the reason behind the attack is a mystery to this day.

CHAPTER 37

BOONE COUNTY'S BASKETBALL REIGN

Although basketball began in Massachusetts, even the inventor of the game conceded that Indiana took the ball and ran with it. Crawfordsville in neighboring Montgomery County hosted the state's first official scheduled basketball game in 1894, and from there interest in the game began to spread rapidly into adjacent towns and counties. Central Indiana, and the area around Boone County in particular, embraced the game with enthusiasm.

When the Indiana High School Athletic Association started its annual high school tournament in 1911, its strongest competitors came from Central Indiana. Teams from Boone County won four out of the first eight years, with adjacent county competitors winning three other championships.

Basketball was likely popular in Indiana because rural teams could easily participate with a minimum of five players. Even in the early years of its inception, the IHSAA restricted teams to seven players. School consolidation helped. IHSAA basketball and the tournament entered the picture at the same time that communities with a one-room schoolhouse and twenty students were being combined into larger schools. Consolidation made these rural areas competitive. One additional contributor to basketball's advancement was the increased availability of the Interurban after the turn of the century. Team travel was facilitated by the quick and efficient network connecting towns with cities. Even college athletics were helped by the existence of the Interurban, with many electing to travel by electric train versus horse and wagon in the 1910s.

When basketball entered the state, there was no officially sanctioned organization governing school athletics. Teachers and superintendents recognized that there needed to be some standards of participation, and by 1903 they agreed to support the formation of the IHSAA. That sealed the progress of basketball's future in Indiana.

Lebanon's high school basketball team started in 1907, when only a handful of high school teams existed. Crawfordsville's school team had been active for eight years, and they were the self-proclaimed champions of high school basketball in Indiana. Their assertion was due to the number of teams they beat, although there was limited competition. In the 1908–9 season, Lebanon's new team finished the season 22–2, with both losses against Crawfordsville. For this reason, the *Lebanon Patriot*, with Strange Cragun as editor, conceded that Crawfordsville must be the true champion of the state.

The following year the two teams were pitted against each other once again. Crawfordsville's record was 13–1, losing only against Lebanon. Lebanon played more games but was left with a slightly lower winning percentage. For this reason, Crawfordsville contended that it should retain its crown as champion. Lebanon refused to concede this self-appointed title and challenged Crawfordsville to a rematch on a neutral court. Crawfordsville declined. Lebanon instead attended the national tournament in Chicago, easily winning the first game and losing the second when a key player suffered a sprained ankle. Their final record was 21–4.

Finally, the IHSAA took steps to create an official solution to the challenge of crowning the best team in the state. In March 1911, it permitted a non-sanctioned twelve-high-school team invitational tournament at Bloomington. The championship game poetically came down to Lebanon versus Crawfordsville, which the latter easily won, becoming the first official high school champions.

Lebanon extracted revenge the next two seasons, when it won back-to-back IHSAA tournaments. Because those tournaments were the first that were formally sanctioned by the IHSAA, the town of Lebanon was recognized as being the first official high school basketball champions in the state. It took nearly fifty years for the IHSAA to publicly recognize Crawfordsville as the first true state champions. It did so at halftime of the 1957 championship game.

Basketball wasn't limited to high school athletes. Starting in the 1900s, many towns had their own basketball clubs, comprising anyone who wanted to play. Sometimes these clubs were organized by local YMCAs or community centers. Thorntown's club team, known as the Americans, was a very organized group, electing officers and a manager and occasionally playing other high schools or colleges.

The Thorntown Americans practiced and played at the local opera house, which had posts in the middle of the room that required maneuvering. When the high school established its own team in 1906, the team tried to use the club court but decided that it posed too much of a challenge. Instead, the team found a location within the high school, a large classroom with low ceilings. Most schools in Central Indiana lacked formal gymnasiums, with teams instead using community rooms, barns with dirt floors or anyplace they could find to play. Lebanon's team played on the second floor of a hotel, in a small room with a stove in the corner. The home teams in these circumstances had a distinct advantage, growing accustomed to making trick shots off the ceiling or a pillar. These teams occasionally faced another challenge: games were known to be canceled when neither team could procure a ball.

Thorntown's high school team continued to improve over the years but didn't make it to the tournament until 1915. They beat Lebanon in the sectionals after losing to them during the regular season. Advancing to the state tournament in Bloomington, they beat Hartford City, Rochester and Manual before facing Montmorenci, a small central Indiana town on the outskirts of Lafayette. Thorntown won 33–10 in the championship game. The team ended their regular season 14–5, averaging 26.4 points per game. Of the seven players on this 1914–15 Thorntown team, only four-year letterman Alfred Smith had previously played on the varsity team. He accounted for approximately 60 percent of the team's total points in the final game. The team was led by Coach Chet Hill, a twenty-two-year-old who had played as a student in high school and college.

After their win, the team paraded back to Thorntown for celebrations. Every business shut its doors, and families lined the streets for a parade led by volunteer musicians. The party shortly turned to upset when Coach Hill discovered that the team's trophy had gone missing. Rumors swirled that it had been stolen by opponents as the team was celebrating and leaving the stadium. To this day, no one knows the fate of the trophy. The coach recognized that his team needed something to commemorate their victory. He acquired the basketballs from the sectional game and the championship game. Cutting each in half, he attached them to a board and carved "State Championship 1915" into the wood. The unofficial trophy is proudly displayed at the Thorntown Heritage Museum.

To replace Thorntown's missing state championship trophy, Coach Chet Hill made one from the game balls. *Author's photo.*

Coach Hill would eventually be inducted into the Indiana Basketball Hall of Fame. His coaching days continued in Martinsville and then Lebanon in 1920 and '21. He was followed by Alfred Smith, who became Lebanon's basketball coach in '21 and '22.

The biggest legacy of the Thorntown championship basketball team was a new urgency to build a gymnasium. It's one early example of a winning team amplifying the need for a new facility to improve their skills. A new gym was completed by the next school year and connected the high school and elementary school buildings. The fans helped to fund the gym, but ironically when construction was completed there was very little seating for spectators.

The other lasting legacy of the 1915 Thorntown team is the community pride. Thorntown High School closed in 1974 when the state began to consolidate smaller school districts, yet the town still celebrates its championship win.

CHAPTER 38

THE BECK TWINS

Zionsville's SullivanMunce Cultural Center, the repository of local history, holds one of the county's most unusual acquisitions. Some consider it the creepiest one.

In 1891 twins Alma and Allie Beck purchased two wreath-making kits from a peddler in order to create their own wreaths made from donated human hair. This wasn't an uncommon practice; in the eighteenth and nineteenth centuries, hair was woven into jewelry as a reminder of deceased relatives. During the Civil War, some soldiers brought bracelets made from their sisters' or mothers' hair as reminders of home.

At the time Alma and Allie were living northwest of Whitestown in the midst of farmland, which makes their ability to collect hair from more than 150 different people more impressive. While not verified, there's a family rumor that the peddler who sold them the wreath spent time in their home that winter and taught the girls how to weave the hair.

To create the wreath, they collected, washed and sorted strands by color. Most who created similar hair wreaths would weave the hair onto forms using hooks similar to crochet hooks. The hair was woven into shapes like flowers, leaves, birds and stems. The finished wreath at the museum is nearly four feet in diameter and has the appearance of being adorned with dried leaves or origami.

The list of those donating hair includes the names of well-known families in the county. Emeline Brock was wife of Pryor Brock and died three years after she donated her hair. Several of the Brock children also contributed to

The Beck twins wove a wreath from hair of family and friends. *Author's photo.*

the wreath. Siblings of Strange Cragun have their hair immortalized, as do many Beck family members and cousins, including those from the Bender family. Even the twins' uncle Abner Beck and his wife, Martha, who lived in eastern Indiana, provided hair.

Allie's wreath was destroyed in a fire. Alma's became an heirloom that hung in various family homes until it was donated to the SullivanMunce Cultural Center by three of her heirs in 1996.

BIBLIOGRAPHY

Anson, Bert. *The Miami Indians*. University of Oklahoma Press, 1970.

Blackburn, Glen A. "Interurban Railroads of Indiana." *Indiana Magazine of History* 20, no. 3 (September 1924).

Boone County Magazine, 1973–86.

Crist, L.M. *History of Boone County*. Indianapolis: A.W. Bowen & Company, 1914.

Esarey, Logan, and George Cottman, eds. "The Building of the Michigan Road." *Indiana Magazine of History* 3–4, 1907. Indiana University Press.

Hanou, John. *A Round Indiana: Round Barns in the Hoosier State*. West Lafayette: Purdue University Press, 2020.

Harden and Spahr. *Early Life and Times in Boone County, Indiana*. Indianapolis: Carlon & Hollenbeck, 1887.

Indianapolis News.

Indianapolis Star.

Krambles, George. *Lebanon-Thorntown Traction Company: The Biography of an Anomaly in "Interurbanland."* Railway & Locomotive Historical Society, 1996.

Lebanon Patriot.

Lebanon Reporter.

Lewis, E.I. "Old Stage-Coach Days." *Indiana Quarterly Magazine of History* (1907).

Marlette, Jerry. *Terre Haute, Indianapolis and Eastern Traction Company*. Indianapolis: Dog Ear, 2011.

Mills, Anson. *My Story*. Washington, D.C.: Press of Byron S. Adams, 1918.

Montgomery, Ethel. "The Building of the Michigan Road." Master's thesis, Purdue University, 1902.

National Register of Historic Places. https://www.nps.gov/subjects/nationalregister/index.htm.

Paddack, Kermit. *Zionsville Basketball: A Century of Eagles.* Self-published, 2016.

A Portrait and Biographical Record of Boone and Clinton Counties, Ind. Chicago: A.W. Bowen, 1895.

Rafert, Stewart. *The Miami Indians of Indiana: A Persistent People.* Indianapolis: Indiana Historical Society, 1996.

Sheets, Harley, and Kermit Paddack. *Tiger Basketball: A Lebanon Passion.* Self-published, 2013.

Zionsville Times Sentinel.

About the Author

Heather Phillips Lusk has always been a writer at heart. After spending decades in marketing, event planning and public relations, she finally returned to her early loves of journalism, history and research. She started by writing for a local newspaper and now is a contributor to various magazines and websites. She and her family reside in Zionsville, in a 120-year-old home with its own story yet to be told.